Story Skills for Managers

Nurturing Motivation with Teams

Tony Wall | Lisa Rossetti

First paperback edition, September 2013.

Printed by CreateSpace (US and Europe).

Design and illustrations by Xavier Caballé Fosch. Background images © Tangient LLC and Photobucket.

British Library Cataloguing-in-Publication Data

A catalogue record for this book is available from the British Library.

ISBN-13: 978-1478191551 (paperback)

ISBN-10: 1478191554 (paperback)

Praise for
Story Skills for Managers

"this book brims with stories that managers can use as is, as well as to inspire their own stories... This reader-friendly and resource-packed volume is destined to be a must-have tool for managers."

> *Katharine Hansen, PhD, Curator, A Storied Career, US.*

"An engaging, user-friendly toolkit for incorporating the power of stories and story-sharing practices into the mindset of a business or non-profit organization."

> *Joseph Daniel Sobol, PhD, East Tennessee State University, Visiting Scholar at the George Ewart Evans Storytelling Research Centre, Wales, and co-founder/editor of Storytelling, Self, Society: An Interdisciplinary Journal of Storytelling Studies.*

"A great tool for all managers who would like some of the most up to date thinking around the value of stories and story telling in the workplace."

> *Andrew Hayward, Senior Consultant in Human Performance Development, AirBusiness Academy, UK.*

"a book that provides tools to reach out to teams by sharing human stories that can touch, motivate and inspire all of us to strive for positive growth both as teams and as individuals."

Scott Cordrey, Senior Manager, multinational retailer, Russia.

"This insightful and timely book is extremely useful and results-focused. Wall and Rossetti successfully draw on their extensive management, coaching and consultancy skills to place stories in their rightful role and place in the managerial and motivational arena. Managers need to read this."

Professor Peter Stokes, awarding winning editor and author, UK Country Director for the EuroMed Business Research Institute and UK Ambassador for the Association Francophone de Gestion des Ressources Humaines (AGRH) (French HR Association).

Acknowledgements

From Tony.

If you believe that as humans we are driven by the desire to feel alive, then I am eternally grateful for all of those people that share their stories with me in my daily life. These people give me life.

If you don't believe that as humans we are driven by the desire to feel alive, then, what might change in your life if you did?

Over the last few years, some special people have left their stories with us on earth without their physical bodies (Nesh, Simon, John and Ron). I will give life to your stories wherever I can, to spread your good intentions and humour.

Did you hear the one about 'Plato and the platypus'? If not... you're missing out!

Tony Wall, Manchester, UK

From Lisa:

People often ask me what first inspired me to develop my interest in the power of stories and my work as a story practitioner. Naturally I had to first be a story listener before becoming a storyteller. Of the many storytellers in my life, my particular thanks go to my paternal grandmother Thirza Ann Callaway, for her legacy of gripping and sometimes downright disturbing family stories in the changing world of Victorian and Edwardian England; to my father for reading me the whole of the extraordinary Tolkien saga at the tender age of seven; and to Prem Rawat for sharing his abundance of wonderful stories that I continue to treasure for their humour and inherent wisdom.

Together, we would like to thank David Somerville for connecting us and helping us shape the book you now see before you. And of course Xavier, who has unlimited patience.

Lisa Rossetti, Chester, UK

Contents

Using this book

Stories are not just a natural way to communicate; they are used to boost engagement and well-being. This books offers managers practical tools and guidance on: how stories keep your finger on the pulse of what's going on; how to design stories to target motivational needs; how to tell high impact stories for optimal effect; and how to breed stories in an upward spiral of positive cultural effect.

This book is designed to be a manager's companion in nurturing the motivation of their team. It has three key parts:

Part 1 – story skills

In the first part, the book introduces stories and story-telling in the context of developing motivation as a manager. It also introduces four key skill areas for developing your story skills: listening, preparing, telling and sharing.

The *introduction* of each of these Chapters provides a short overview of that skill area. It is kept short for your quick and easy access.

At the end of each Chapter, there are two areas for you to develop your skill:

- *Key questions*, to deepen your knowledge and skills about the particular skill area.

- *Key action points*, which *you* will think of, to encourage you to actively commit to manageable actions which will further deepen your skills and create organisational impacts.

Throughout, you will find blank templates of tools which we want you to use – we want you to write and scribble in this book!

Part 2 - stories for motivation

In the second part, the book provides a collation of powerful stories that can be used by managers in their team contexts. These can be used in multiple situations and circumstances, depending on the motivational aim (see the Chapter on *Preparing Stories*).

It is essential that you read, as a minimum, the Chapters on *Preparing* and *Telling Stories* before you read these stories in any context. Context is critical to optimise the impact of stories.

Following the stories, there are a variety of reflective questions to stimulate reflection.

These can be personal reflections for the storyteller (the manager), or used with the team. You may use all of them, one or two of them, or make up your own.

We also encourage you to prepare your own stories to ensure a fit with the context in which you want to use them.

You may feel you are not creative – but as you will read in the introduction, storytelling is as much a left brain activity as it is a right brain one!

Part 3 – resources

In the final part, we provide you with a variety of additional readings and viewings which you might find useful. We encourage you to explore video and imagery as well as texts.

We hope you enjoy your experience of reading and applying your learning from this book... we hope you see the same transformative effects we see in our own work from telling stories.

Introducing stories

Introducing stories: overview and key points

Stories are over 100,000 years old and some scientists think that this is the reason that our brains are wired in the way they are. But stories are not just a natural way to communicate, they can be used to inspire and motivate people to do great things. Managers can tap into the motivational force of stories in ways that boost engagement and well-being.

The key points of this Chapter are:

- Our brains are wired in ways that mean we instinctually make sense of the world through stories.

- Motivating in ways which create anxiety and stress is not sustainable – but we *can* focus on psychological states which boost drive whilst maintaining well-being.

- We can use this information to design and deliver stories for optimal motivational impact.

100,000 years old

Humans have been telling stories for over 100,000 years. Stories explained the world, created bonds within social groups and identified us with our ancestors and origins through tales of heroes and epic journeys. We used stories to teach morals, customs and values to our young so that they could take their place in those earliest of societies.

In modern times, the oral telling of folk tales persists across Africa, Australasia, India and beyond. Folk tales are not told for nostalgia nor to satisfy the tourist palette.

> Story tellers serve basic needs in society

Storytellers are still serving the basic needs of human groups, to be motivated to work harmoniously and bravely together, to have hurts and confusion healed, to be inspired towards greater or more ethical things and perhaps to be transformed in our thinking and being.

The power of stories endures to this day and it is perhaps most for its motivational quality that storytelling is rapidly gaining credence in the 21st century workplace.

The rise of social media, from Facebook to tweeting to blogging, suggests that people are returning to "narrative knowing" to reclaim a sense of personal power by "storying" life events into meaning and order (Tercek, 2011).

> **>We create who we are through story**

In other words, I become something meaningful when I create stories about what I am doing and what I am thinking (@writing-a-book-right-now). And this feels good.

A growing science

Since the 1990s researchers investigating behaviour in organisations have acknowledged anecdotal evidence and personal narrative as valid data for organisational analysis, for their ability to 'open windows' into the cultural, political and emotional lives of organisations (see Gabriel 2008, 2009).

In the early 2000s, Lewis, Amini and Lannon (2001) reported scientific research which found that our brain chemistry and nervous systems are measurably affected by those closest to us.

They found that our ability to relate to each other meaningfully which is inherent in our brain's geography (what they call 'limbic resonance') is enhanced by the language and medium of stories.

We then heard from the evolutionary biologists who say that storytelling as the dominant form of social and organisational interaction has hardwired the human brain towards stories as a sense-making and socialising process (Haven, 2007).

And by 2013, we hear neuroscientists (brain researchers) saying similar things: that the brain is 'hard-wired' to represent and make sense of reality through story-telling, as a kind of innate instinct (Pace-Schott, 2013). We find this profound.

> **>We are hard-wired to live through story**

Yet we also know that there is a prevailing belief in the metaphor of the left brain vs right brain, which constrains storytelling to a creative 'right brained' activity for 'creative people' (Jarrett, 2012). This is a stumbling block for many managers to get on board with storytelling.

Counter to this belief, split brain research actually reveals that it is the *left* hemisphere of the brain which is the interpreter and narrator, making sense of life's situations – whereas the *right* hemisphere enjoys the story as a way of processing emotions and understanding others (Jarrett, 2012). Story is, therefore, a whole brain, whole person activity.

A powerful force

Stories, sagas and myths have motivated our hunters to collectively face danger, overcome the odds and ensure the survival of our race. Might stories continue to be a vital motivational force in human organisation and performance today?

The Harvard Business Review, Wall Street Journal, CIO Magazine, The World Bank, NASA, Bristol Myers Squib, IBM, Disney, Ford and even the US Defense Advanced Research Projects Agency (DARPA) all endorse storytelling as a motivational force.

Steve Denning is one of the most prominent thought leaders who advocates organisational storytelling as a leadership competence. He claims that a deep understanding of narrative is key to transformational leadership (Denning, 2007).

He goes further to say that the secret to building successful teams is to use storytelling in everyday business practice:

> Narrative stimulates high-performance teams and communities to participate with passion (Denning 2011: 160).

Nurturing motivation is a key aspect of developing such high-performing teams. **And by 'motivation', we are specifically talking about a state of mind that drives people in ways that maintains their sense of well-being.**

Neuropsychologists can help us understand this in more detail. A key theme emerging from brain science over the last decade or so is the overarching organising principle of maximising reward and minimising threat (Gordon, 2000).

In other words:

- we work ***towards*** things (pleasure), or we

- work ***away*** from things (pain).

(Though we also now know that there is another response – paralysis – where we keep still until we are out of the situation we think caused it).

This organising principle is a major influence on how we make decisions or behave and can apply to all aspects and areas of our lives, because it is part of the 'hard-wiring' of the brain (Dixon, Rock and Ochsner, 2010).

Though *away* states are powerful, we know that over time, they create high levels of stress, and our perception and decision making capabilities are noticeably reduced (see Rock, 2008). In turn, that can and does affect the well-being of team members.

Imagine the scenario of always running away from a threat; think of the endless running in the Terminator movies and TV series. Over time, people get stressed, tired, angry, upset, and mistakes are made. The behaviour is driven by a push to action.

On the other hand, *towards* states are conducive to a much more balanced and more fulfilling work life. They too are powerful in driving behaviour, but

> **>States affect our openness and well-being**

provide a psychological environment which can enhance perception, problem solving and decision-making (see Rock, 2008).

In other words, people can be significantly more open to receiving key messages that we want to offer our team members, and turning it in to behaviour.

Imagine the scenario of a volunteer who works with abandoned pets. He absolutely loves his work volunteering. He gets to work on-time every day, never misses a day off work, and is well regarded by his peers and patients alike. He does a good job. He is driven by the satisfaction he gets by doing his job. The behaviour is driven by a pull, or attraction.

> **Being driven *towards* is a powerful state**

But how do the towards and away states relate to stories? Well, to answer this, reflect on the following questions:

- Have you ever heard a story that put you in a bad mood? That angered you? That made you feel like going home? For example, a story about your big boss getting a pay rise in a time when everybody else is having their pay frozen?

- Have you ever heard stories that made you feel *less* angry or upset about a situation; maybe the big boss had their comeuppance? Or maybe you heard a story about how much of a contribution you had personally made?

- Have you ever heard a story that made you feel top of the world, or inspired and energised you? For example, a story about how a colleague helps another colleague in a difficult situation?

- Or have you ever listened to a story and not even realised it had affected you? Of course this is a trick question – you wouldn't know! But believe us, these are all around us, working day and night.

Stories have direct affects in creating towards and away states, as implied in these questions. To know how stories can work in these ways, we draw on brain science research.

For Rock (2008), there are five key 'domains of experience' that can activate both **towards** or **away** states – summarised by the acronym SCARF on the next page.

Status	Is about one's sense of importance in relation to others.
Certainty	Is about one's sense of being able to predict the future.
Autonomy	Is about one's sensed ability to control events.
Relatedness	Is about one's sense of safety with others, or a feeling that an interaction is with more of a friend than a foe.
Fairness	Is about one's sense of being treated fairly in any exchanges (communication, decision making, etc.).

(Source: based on Rock, 2008).

So stories can heighten the motivational forces of the team, or specific team members within it, through a creative, open and productive ***towards*** state.

They can do this by communicating messages about:

- The importance of the team (or specific team members) in relation to others,

- What's going to happen next (or not),

- How the team (or specific team members within it) can make decisions about how things can be,

- Feeling safe within the team (and with you),

- Being treated fairly,

- *Any* or *all* of the above.

But stories can also heighten the motivational forces of an individual through a threatening and stressful ***away*** state. They can do this by communicating messages about:

- Being less important than other areas of the organisation,

- Uncertainty about what's going to happen,

- How decisions are (or need to be) made elsewhere,

- Not appreciating the need for healthy relationships within the team (and with you),

- Being treated unfairly,

- *Any* or *all* of the above.

The point is that both types of stories motivate behaviour – but our crucial point is that **we are specifically talking about enabling a state of mind that drives people in ways that maintains their sense of well-being.**

>A state of mind that drives in ways that maintains well-being

The rest of this book is dedicated to helping you build your skills towards this task.

Now, complete the reflective questions and actions points over the next few pages.

We will provide these at the end of each Chapter.

Key questions for now:

1. For you, what is the most significant fact about stories or storytelling from this Chapter?

2. What is the most motivating story you have ever heard? What was it about? How did it affect you?

3. What stories do you habitually tell about the workforce, management, customers? Do they work to put people in a towards or away state?

4. Thinking about your context:

    a. Which teams do you have a leadership role in?

    b. Which team or individuals might benefit the most from motivational boosts?

    c. Which team or individuals might be a useful 'test-bed' for you to share your new story ideas and practices?

My key action points:

Now commit to three action points from this Chapter, by writing them here:

1.

2.

3.

References

Denning, S. (2007) *The Secret Language of Leadership: How Leaders Inspire Action through Narrative,* San Francisco, CA: Jossey Bass.

Denning, S. (2011) *The Leader's Guide to Storytelling: Mastering the Art and Discipline of Business Narrative,* San Francisco, CA: John Wiley and Sons.

Dixon, P., Rock, D. and Ochsner, K. (2010) Turn the 360 Around, *NeuroLeadership Journal,* Issue 3.

Gabriel, Y. (2008) *Organizing Words: A Critical Thesaurus for Social and Organization Studies,* Oxford: Oxford University Press.

Gabriel, Y. (2009) *Research Resources: Organizational Seminar Series. http://www.organizational-storytelling.org.uk/research-resources/storytelling-in-organizations/.*

Gordon, E. (2000) *Integrative Neuroscience: Bringing together Biological, Psychological and Clinical Models of the Human Brain,* Singapore: Harwood Academic Publishers.

Haven, K. (2007) *Story Proof: the science behind the startling power of story*, Westport, CN: Libraries Unlimited.

Jarrett, C. (2012) Brain Myths: Why the Left-Brain Right-Brain Myth Will Probably Never Die, *Psychology Today*, 27th June, available at http://www.psychologytoday.com/blog/brain-myths/201206/why-the-left-brain-right-brain-myth-will-probably-never-die. Accessed 25th July 2013.

Lewis, T., Amini, F. and Lannon, R. (2001) *A General Theory of Love*, New York: Random House.

Pace-Schott, E.F. (2013) Dreaming as a Story-Telling Instinct, *Frontiers in Psychology*, 4, 149, doi: 10.3389/fpsyg.2013.00159.

Rock, D. (2008) SCARF: a brain-based model for collaborating with and influencing others, *NeuroLeadership Journal*, Issue 1.

Tercek, R. (2011) TED Talk: Reclaiming The Power of Personal Narrative, http://tedxtalks.ted.com/video/TEDxMarin-Robert-Tercek-Reclaim.

Listening to stories

Listening to stories: overview and key points

Team members tell stories which are real time, in the moment, and hold nuggets of information which can aid management decision making and action. Listening to stories gives managers timely information about what might need to happen, in terms of motivation or wider, and gives direction as to what stories to craft, tell and share more broadly, and how and when to do it.

The key points of this Chapter are that:

- Listening out for stories gives us a 'finger on the pulse' of our team to know what's going on, right now.

- Listening to certain elements of stories gives us a rich set of information which informs decision making.

- Listening for patterns is crucial to decide when to act and when to continue listening – some stories happen by chance or by coincidence.

Your finger on the pulse

We seem to be hearing more horror stories of employees knowing how (badly) an organisation is performing before it reaches news headlines. Horror stories of banks investing in massively high risk areas, of certain hospitals providing deathly poor care, and of mines bursting into flames.

It is no coincidence that in each case, employees knew or had concerns about what was going on, as they saw it – in real time. They told the story from their perspective, usually spurred on

> **>Stories exist before news head-lines**

by connecting with the stories of others. They, themselves, were spotting patterns beyond their own anecdotal experience.

For managers at all levels, an incredibly powerful skill is listening to these stories that are always around us. They provide timely information about what is going on – and this is not just about the doom and gloom (though this does tend to have dramatic effect in stories). It is also about what's going well, who's doing well, and why.

An expression we use on a daily basis is to 'listen out'; we listen out for the door-bell or listen out for the phone. So too, should we listen out for the stories around us. The *'out'* is important; it is outside of us, and all around us.

Whether a horror or feel-good story, listening out for the stories around us gives us rich, real time information about what we might be doing differently in relation to motivation, or wider afield.

Stories abound in organisations at all levels; the trick is to be a good story listener. A good **>Stories live all around us** place to start is with personal stories. Most people are telling stories quite naturally on an everyday basis but probably without the intentional and honed purpose that a motivational story requires.

Listening out is about having a finger on the pulse of your team, and what's happening from their perspective. But what specifically can we listen out for?

What to listen out for

There are different ways of thinking about the elements of stories, but we have adapted some user-friendly questions from contemporary research (see Crabtree, Alber-Morgan and Konrad, 2010, and Holley and Colyar, 2012).

With respect to a story being told, the questions are:

1. When and where is it taking place?

2. Who are the main characters?

3. What are the problems or conflicts?

4. How are the problems or conflicts resolved (if they are)?

5. What is the story about?

6. From whose point of view is it being told?

Here is some guidance about each of the elements, with some examples of each.

When and where is it taking place?

This is the setting, context or location of the story. For example, what time of the day, week or year is being mentioned? Which particular departments or teams are being mentioned as the context of the story?

Who are the main characters?

These are the people (or organisations or objects) that have a role to play in the story. For example, which specific team members are being mentioned? Which particular customers or service users are being mentioned?

What are the problems or conflicts?

These are the key messages about something that needs to be resolved in a story. For example, what are struggles, battles or challenges being mentioned? What are the key sources of difference between the characters mentioned above? Importantly, what are the motivational elements can you spot related to status, certainty, autonomy, relatedness and fairness?

How are the problems or conflicts resolved (if they are)?

These are the solutions to the problems or conflicts. For example, how are the struggles, battles or challenges mentioned overcome? How are the key sources of difference between the characters overcome? Sometimes there isn't a resolution which can create a state of discomfort or anxiety. Sometimes, this can aim to keep the status quo (you'll also read about Refrain Stories later on in the *Preparing Stories* Chapter). Again, what do the stories say about the resolution in terms of the motivational elements of status, certainty, autonomy, relatedness and fairness?

What is the story about?

This is the main message about the story, or the moral of the story. It is that 'special something' that is to be learnt from the story. This is usually communicated as a result of all other aspects of the story. For example, is it about how we *should* behave in certain circumstances, how we *should* think about something, or how we should *feel* about something?

From whose point of view is it being told?

This is about whose perspective the story is being told from. Is it the individual telling the story? Is it told from the perspective of a group (e.g. 'we', 'us', 'them', 'accounts', 'marketing', 'HR', etc)? Or is it told as if it was an objective statement, 'this is the way it is'?

This *can* give you insight into the *source* of the story or information within it – is it from the people implicated by the story, or another perspective? (e.g. is it about what employees think of their own performance, or how HR see their performance?). It can also help you decipher how *widespread* the story teller thinks the issue is – is it one-off or consistent?

Let's take an example.

Example 1

You are in a team meeting and one of your team members comments on a new system that you have to implement:

> *I've heard about that new customer relationship management system HR want us to use – they've been wanting to implement it for a lifetime. A slug is faster and nobody is going to use it...*

> *It's just like the time HR spent all that money on those fancy computers which could detect when you needed a coffee [laughs]... they didn't work and nobody used it.*

> *We're better sticking to our own current system that we know works...*

On the next page, make notes about your key thoughts about this narrative.

When and where is it taking place?

Who are the main characters?

What are the problems or conflicts?

How are the problems or conflicts resolved (if they are)?

What is the story about?

From whose point of view is it being told?

Some elements that we might pick out are outlined below:

When and where is it taking place?
- *Now, and 'last time'.*

Who are the main characters?
- *HR*
- *We/us*

What are the problems or conflicts?
- *HR want to implement a new system but the new system is slow.*

How are the problems or conflicts resolved (if they are)?
- *Last time: nobody used the system.*
- *This time: do the same.*

What is the story about?
- *HR repeatedly not knowing what we/us need, and how to resolve the problem.*

From whose point of view is it being told?
- *Those implicated by the new system (we/us).*

Now let's take another example.

Example 2

Choose one of the stories from this book and identify some of the most important elements of the story. Think specifically about what it says about motivation, and how to motivate.

When and where is it taking place?

Who are the main characters?

What are the problems or conflicts?

How are the problems or conflicts resolved (if they are)?

What is the story about?

From whose point of view is it being told?

Looking for patterns

If we are always surrounded – or even bombarded – by stories, how do we possibly digest all of them? Can't we become overloaded? The skill is not about digesting all of the stories, nor all of their elements. Rather, it is about keeping an open enough mind to spot patterns in the stories, which can then inform what you decide to do next.

One proverb that provides a useful way of deciding whether to act on particular elements of stories or not, is based on distinguishing between chance, coincidence and pattern. If something occurs:

1. Once, it can be by **chance**

2. Twice, it can be **coincidence**

3. Three times, it is a **pattern.**

So if you hear an aspect of a story occurring **once**, it might be something not to address or notice in future conversations (note: of course this depends on the relative importance of it, such as a health and safety incident).

The **second** time you hear something, it is worth noting, and perhaps listening out for similar stories. Yet it could still be a coincidence.

The **third** time is likely to be a pattern, so is likely to require some action, whether it is related to motivation or not. The focus of this book primarily relates to how you, as a manager, can nurture motivation in teams, but it is important not to ignore other patterns you spot. It is not that these wider patterns can boost performance, they can save lives too.

Let's return to the earlier example (about the new slug-speed system that HR want to implement), from the angle of motivation. Over time, you might have picked up a number of patterns, for example:

- What is the story about? HR repeatedly not knowing what we/us need, and how to resolve the problem.

- How are the problems or conflicts resolved (if they are)? Last time: nobody used the system. This time: do the same.

- Who are the main characters? HR and 'we/us'.

In terms of the motivational elements of SCARF, the patterns in the stories indicate that the following may need attention (of course, you might pick out other elements – but which do you feel are the strongest in your context?):

Relatedness: there is a feeling of disconnect between HR and 'we/us'. So, what might be done to close this gap? What stories can be told about a *partnership* between the team and HR?

Autonomy: the lack in relatedness may have resulted from HR not involving the team in the decision making around what system the team should be using – or how they use it. So what might be done to enhance aspects of autonomy in relation to the system? What stories might be told about this autonomy, even though it might be limited?

Certainty: as a result of not being involved in the systems that the team operate, and this happening over time, there is a sense that the team does not know what is coming next, and want to keep the (certainty) of the existing system. So, what might be done to enhance certainty around the system? What stories can be told which will enhance a feeling of certainty?

As shown above, once you have spotted patterns in the stories your team members tell, this can inform what you do next. There may be multiple SCARF elements that need to be addressed; that is to be expected. But as a starting point, which do you feel are the strongest?

In turn, this will also include deciphering which stories you prepare, tell and share with your team to address motivational elements of SCARF. The following Chapters about *Preparing, Telling and Sharing Stories* offer your next steps in building your story skills to nurture motivation.

In the meantime, we provide some blank story elements tools on the next few pages to help you listen out for stories in your workplace.

Story Elements Tool

Use the following table to jot your own notes of some of the stories in your own context.

When and where is it taking place?

Who are the main characters?

What are the problems or conflicts?

How are the problems or conflicts resolved (if they are)?

What is the story about?

From whose point of view is it being told?

Story Elements Tool

Use the following table to jot your own notes of some of the stories in your own context.

When and where is it taking place?

Who are the main characters?

What are the problems or conflicts?

How are the problems or conflicts resolved (if they are)?

What is the story about?

From whose point of view is it being told?

Story Elements Tool

Use the following table to jot your own notes of some of the stories in your own context.

When and where is it taking place?

Who are the main characters?

What are the problems or conflicts?

How are the problems or conflicts resolved (if they are)?

What is the story about?

From whose point of view is it being told?

Key questions for now:

1. What stories are you aware of in your own team context right now?

2. What are the key elements of the stories you can hear around you in your team?

3. Listen out for stories told during one day (today or tomorrow) – what are the patterns you can spot?

4. Listen out for stories told during one week (this week) – what are the patterns you can spot?

5. What actions might you need to take after spotting these patterns?

My key action points:

Now commit to three action points from this Chapter, by writing them here:

1.

2.

3.

References

Crabtree, T., Alber-Morgan, S. R. and Konrad, M., (2010) "The Effects of Self-Monitoring of Story Elements on the Reading Comprehension of High School Seniors with Learning Disabilities", *Education and Treatment of Children*, Vol. 33, No. 2, pp. 187-203.

Holley, K. and Colyar, J. (2012) "Under Construction: How Narrative Elements Shape Qualitative Research", *Theory into Practice*, Vol. 51, No. 2, pp. 114-121.

Preparing stories

Preparing stories: overview and key points

Attentively listening to stories provides useful information about the motivational needs and issues of team members. For managers, this is key to intentionally preparing stories to target their motivational efforts and energies. Knowing the AIMM of a story, before it is told or shared, helps managers to optimise the positive motivational impact they want to achieve with their team.

The key points of this Chapter are that:

- Knowing the motivational needs or issues to be addressed can help focus efforts and energies.

- Being clear about the Audience, Intent, Message and Moment can help managers select or write a story to optimise its impact.

- Knowing the different story types can help managers know which story to select or write.

Stories for a useful direction

As we said in the *Listening to Stories* Chapter, stories are all around us; they are told on a daily basis. But books, magazines, and the Internet are also great places to unearth stories.

Current events make for good stories if they are relevant to your team's needs, but remember that simply repeating the news without considering your story's message and purpose is a pointless conversation.

Imagine the scenario of a manager, Karen, holding a monthly team meeting to review the progress of a project. There is some good progress with most of the milestones, but there are some other areas, namely budget, that are off target.

Karen decides to tell a story to motivate the team to make changes to get back on target. That's perfectly plausible so far; people do this every day in organisations.

Karen opts to tell a personal, childhood story. A story that is about how she had fallen off her cycle when she was aged 8, grazed a knee and lost a tooth. Karen proceeds to talk about her friends – and all of the shortcomings of her friends...

Her friends didn't tell her about the tree in front of her, her friends didn't help fast enough, her friends didn't help her clean her wounds afterwards... (We ask: what type of friends are these?!).

The memory is authentic, so Karen feels the anger and resentment towards her friends return. Karen continues and makes eye contact with team members who she thinks are to blame (not consciously, but the anger is oozing out of her).

After telling her story, Karen starts to notice how her team has recoiled in to their seats, smiles have turned to frowns, and she gets the sense that people are feeling uncomfortable.

They are – they feel like the friends that Karen is talking about!

> **>Stories will impact, but is it the impact you want?**

Congratulations, the story has had impact... but just not the one Karen wanted! She has probably put people in an *away* state; they may be spurred into action (leaving the room?) by affecting their SCARF.

It is likely these SCARF elements have been affected:

- Status: even though the message was indirect, the message appeared to blame certain individuals for not hitting the budget targets, and therefore questioned individual team member performance and abilities.

- Relatedness: Karen appeared to be criticising / blaming an individual in a public arena, and in turn, has potentially upset her relationship with the specific individual and their relationship with the wider team.

- Fairness: was public criticism of individual performance and ability necessary or fair?

It is crucial that managers are crystal clear about why they are telling the story, in terms of nurturing the motivation of their teams. And clearly in this case, the telling of the story was just as important as the story that was selected to be shared. This is discussed in more depth in the *Telling Stories* Chapter next.

Simmons (2007) reminds us that stories must be *mindfully* told to create the results managers want in a workplace. This partly means selecting a story with a purpose (or intent), which is relevant to the situation.

> **>Being mindful about what you are trying to achieve**

AIMMing

The basic 'AIM' model is a popular acronym for the key aspects of presenting information to people in a variety of contexts. It reflects modern writers (see, for example, Theobold, 2011), but is in a practical and easy to use format.

But this is not enough, and we propose an extension of 'AIM' to what we will call 'AIMM', which stands for:

- Audience

- Intent

- Message

- Moment.

There are various versions of this model, and we suggest you use one you feel comfortable with. We use the above version of AIMM in this book.

To use stories to purposively motivate others in particular directions, it is useful to know what direction you are seeking to travel in. This is about understanding the motivational need of the team or individuals within in.

Within the previous Chapter, we discussed the use of spotting patterns in the stories you hear – these will provide the essence of the motivational need. And they will tend to form around SCARF (see the *Introducing Stories* and *Listening to Stories* Chapters):

- Status

- Certainty

- Autonomy

- Relatedness

- Fairness.

This, for us, then influences the key elements of the story or stories you decide to select (or write) before telling them.

So bringing AIMM and SCARF together might look like the table on the next page.

Audience	Who will be listening? What is their current motivational state? What will they be expecting? What might be at the edge of possibility*?
Intent	Which motivational element(s) of SCARF are you trying to address?
Message	Which specific motivational message (in relation to SCARF) are you trying to communicate?
Moment**	When (time) should it be delivered to optimise the desired effect? Where (location) should it be delivered to optimise the desired effect?

*The idea of the 'edge of possibility' is an important concept. Others refer to it as being on the edge of somebody's 'mental map of the world'. In other words, it is about what is currently seen as acceptable or possible from an individual's understanding of the world.

An example might be a team member who fundamentally *believes* they cannot work in partnership with the HR function. If they hold this belief, any direct messages which attempt to suggest working in partnership will be rejected – or potentially worse – stimulate an overt reaction which is then communicated around the wider team.

> **>Start within the edge of possibility, and then move outwards**

The edge of possibility, as a first step towards closer working, might not be "working in partnership" with HR, but "enhancing communications" with HR.

Over time, when the person experiences "enhanced communications", the edge of possibility can expand. From there, you can edge outwards again, in a constant edging-outwards movement.

For these reasons, it is important in the telling of any story that the AIMM is known upfront, and that the effects of the story are closely monitored to ensure optimal effect for motivation.

**A further note: the Moment aspect is more related to the telling of the story, and so this will be discussed in more depth in the *Telling Stories* Chapter. It is an important aspect to mention here, however, as a key aspect of the design of a story.

Example of AIMMing at SCARF

The motivational need might infiltrate one or all of aspects of AIMM. Let's refer back to the example from the *Listening to Stories* Chapter. In this example, you are in a team meeting and one of your team members comments on a new system that you have to implement.

But you find, after listening to your team's stories, and spotting wider patterns, that this is just one example of a story where the main characters are HR and 'we/us', that the stories are about HR repeatedly not knowing what we/us need, and that this problem is best resolved by nobody using the system.

In terms of the motivational elements of SCARF, you may decide that the following may need attention:

- Relatedness: to address a feeling of disconnect between HR and 'we/us'.

- Autonomy: the lack in relatedness may have resulted from HR not involving the team in the decision making around what system the team should be using – or how they use it.

- Certainty: as a result of not being involved in the systems that the team operate, and this happening over time, there is a sense that the team does not know what is coming next, and want to keep the (certainty of the) existing system.

So, this gives you some direction and some options about the AIMM of your story.

In relation to the example above, have a go at jotting down some AIMM ideas in the table on the next few pages. We will offer you our thoughts afterwards.

Audience

Who will be listening?

What is their current motivational state?

What will they be expecting?

What might be at the edge of possibility?

Intent

Which motivational element(s) of SCARF are you trying to address?

Message

Which specific motivational message (in relation to SCARF) are you trying to communicate?

Moment

When (time) should it be delivered to optimise the desired effect?

Where (location) should it be delivered to optimise the desired effect?

Here are some of our thoughts about the earlier example.

Audience

Who will be listening:

My team members. Mixed ages. Different experience levels.

What is their current motivational state:

Friday morning, so energy levels low. However, disgruntled at HR.

What will they be expecting:

Usual monthly team meeting which reviews performance of the team.

What might be at the edge of possibility:

In terms of the patterns from my story listening: trying to get autonomy will be difficult – that aspect is hard to change right now. Same with certainty. Trying to get a partnership between the team and HR would also be difficult, but 'enhancing communications' might be more acceptable.

Intent

Which motivational element(s) of SCARF
are you trying to address:

**I would specifically like to
address relatedness through the
story.**

Message

Which specific motivational message (in
relation to SCARF) are you trying to
communicate:

**I would specifically like to
address relatedness through the
specific message of "working
together achieves more".**

Moment

When (time) should it be delivered to
optimise the desired effect:

**At the team meeting. This is
where it relates to working with
HR most significantly. But I can
also reinforce over time on an
individual, one-to-one basis.**

Where (location) should it be delivered
to optimise the desired effect:

> **In the team office, and I shall sit
> alongside people, rather than at
> the head of the table so I am not
> directing the message at any one
> single individual.**

The AIMM tool gives you the parameters
from which to select or write a story. In the
above example, it might be that versions of
"*Anansi the Spider*" (Parts 1 or 2) or "*Stone
Soup*" might be told. They both have clear
messages around people bringing different
strengths or ingredients to the table.

But remember the *Audience* – what are they
expecting? To burst forth into stories about
spiders or soup could have disastrous
consequences – especially in the context of
the above situation, with this specific AIMM.

Yet, if the situation is carefully set up, where
people are in an open enough, receptive
state to listen to a story, then this would be
powerful. If not, and their state is noticeably
'disgruntled', then a literal story from
personal experience might be more
powerful and acceptable within the
situation.

We talk more about this in the next Chapter, *Telling Stories*, but the last aspect to consider here is the type of stories to tell, as part of the AIMM.

Types of stories

Simmons (2007) says that telling a story from a real-life situation engages, and so sharing your own successes and failures with your team can engender trust in your human side. But whether it is personal or not, Simmons suggests that there are six types of story:

- ***Who I Am*** stories give a glimpse of what motivates you and engenders trust in you. For example, it could be a story about your motivation to give *autonomy* to the team, or to *delegate* rather than *instruct*.

- ***Why I Am Here*** are transparent "come clean" stories when you have an achievement to share or even bad news to convey. For example, it might be about how you had helped a team transform itself at a previous organisation.

- The **Vision Story** paints a compelling picture and connects with others about a future state of being or achievement. For example, to be the best performing team in the organisation. Or to have the highest satisfaction rates. But beware of this type of story becoming too corny (or cheesy or clichéd).

- **Teaching Stories** help listeners understand the benefits of certain behaviours and values. Folk tales, personal stories and many of the stories presented in this book fall in to this category. For example, the story *"Stone Soup"* in this book might be seen to be about how individuals can pool their strengths together for greater, wider benefit.

- The **Values in Action** story demonstrates what you, your team or your organisation stand for; these stories are best drawn from real life. For example, a team may need to value integrity, equality and creativity together. The story *"A Personal Philosophy of Facilitation"* in this book falls into this category.

- *I Know What You're Thinking* stories voice your team members' fears and concerns rather than glossing over or avoiding. This type of story helps people come to terms with potential changes in their situation and status like the dissolution of teams, redundancy or even promotion, and helps them deal with uncertainty. This is particularly useful for addressing motivational issues related to the Certainty element of SCARF. It is also useful for reframing complaints in to opportunities for resolution and action.

A note about 'refrain stories'

People who work therapeutically with stories identify certain stories, like the one about HR's sluggish IT system, as Refrain Stories. These stories are more often than not unresolved; that is, they have no resolution or conclusion.

Refrain Stories in the workplace are likely to be complaints about a situation ("HR doesn't understand us"). Their power lies in the affirming of Status, Certainty and Relatedness. We all believe that we are the victims of HR's attitude towards us; thus we know where we stand.

However even though the constant repeating of a Refrain Story is an attempt to make sense of a current situation, it never helps us to move on and resolve the conflict or problem. It is rather like a car engine which never quite turns over no matter how many times you turn the key.

If you decide to address a Refrain Story, you will need a "re-framing" story which offers a more positive perspective and contains a resolution or call to action of some kind.

We provide some blank AIMM Story Preparation sheets on the next few pages for you to use, before you tell or share stories. Though not a requirement to tell or share stories, we believe using this tool will help you hone your skills in selecting and writing stories for optimal impact.

AIMM Story Preparation Tool

Audience
Who will be listening?

What is their current motivational state?

What will they be expecting?

What might be at the edge of possibility?

Intent
Which motivational element(s) of SCARF are you trying to address?

Message

Which specific motivational message (in relation to SCARF) are you trying to communicate?

Moment

When (time) should it be delivered to optimise the desired effect?

Where (location) should it be delivered to optimise the desired effect?

AIMM Story Preparation Tool

Audience
Who will be listening?

What is their current motivational state?

What will they be expecting?

What might be at the edge of possibility?

Intent
Which motivational element(s) of SCARF are you trying to address?

Message

Which specific motivational message (in relation to SCARF) are you trying to communicate?

Moment

When (time) should it be delivered to optimise the desired effect?

Where (location) should it be delivered to optimise the desired effect?

AIMM Story Preparation Tool

Audience
Who will be listening?

What is their current motivational state?

What will they be expecting?

What might be at the edge of possibility?

Intent
Which motivational element(s) of SCARF are you trying to address?

Message

Which specific motivational message (in relation to SCARF) are you trying to communicate?

Moment

When (time) should it be delivered to optimise the desired effect?

Where (location) should it be delivered to optimise the desired effect?

Key questions for now:

1. Which stories have you heard where any of the AIMM aspects were inappropriate?

2. Which stories have you heard where the AIMM aspects were well prepared?

3. What were the key motivational needs you identified from the previous Chapter that need addressing?

4. What story AIMM may you need to do over the next week? Do an AIMM analysis before you tell or share a story.

5. What story type might that AIMM need?

My key action points:

Now commit to three action points from this Chapter, by writing them here:

1.

2.

3.

References

Gallo, C. (2010) *The presentation secrets of Steve Jobs: how to be insanely great in front of any audience*, London: McGraw-Hill.

Simmons, A. (2007) *Whoever Tells the Best Story Wins*, New York: Amacom.

Theobald, T. (2011) *Develop your presentation skills*, London: Kogan Page.

Telling stories

Telling stories: overview and key points

In this Chapter, we will take a look at the skill of choosing and telling a story to motivate your team, and in particular the What, How, and Where of story-telling. We will look at the environment of storytelling and some techniques to optimise the power of stories to influence the motivational needs of others. Finally, the accompanying key questions will help you build your story telling skills within your organisation.

The key points of this Chapter are:

- Introduce storytelling into your work place carefully to enable your team to adjust its thinking style.

- Traditional stories and film directors can teach us how to structure our stories, with a clear beginning, middle and end.

- Make use of metaphors and other story techniques for maximum effect.

Choosing or creating the right moment

At first sight, our modern fast-paced business world is not an ideal environment for telling stories. Small wonder managers are inclined to view storytelling as the responsibility of leaders at the 'Annual General Meeting' or Christmas party. Luckily you don't have to be a seasoned after-dinner speaker to tell a really effective motivational story.

Nor are microphones, stages, and strange storytelling hats required! As we have alluded to through the AIMM model in the *Preparing Stories* Chapter, we need to create appropriate Moments to tell stories. The environment needs to permit engaged listening and trust. It is also useful to minimise distractions to maximise focus.

Perhaps the biggest obstacle to using storytelling is the thinking styles prevalent in the world of business. Stories require us to unhook from the need for justification and "proof", from linear and root-cause thinking, from the authority of our charts, metrics and spreadsheets.

> **>You have the choice to use story every day**

It is a question of training your brain to be more flexible so that you can discern when and with whom a story is a more appropriate and effective communication, shifting from one communication mode to another.

Let's take an example.

James is preparing his team's monthly report. Up until now, he simply reads out a list of targets met and worryingly more frequently *not* met by his team.

Although the team regularly attends these meetings, they are pretty lacklustre and people make few comments or contributions.

James decides he will include a story to motivate his team. He prepares a story from his own life, about a time when he had to try and try again to achieve something (see "*Light My Fire*" as an example).

He is hoping that the team will take heart and even though targets are below expectations they will renew their efforts.

He launches into "Let me tell you a story..." and gets alarmed expressions.

What went wrong? Unfortunately, he had not prepared the team to switch their usual thinking style.

This threatened their Certainty (SCARF) about the usual monthly meetings. They also feel confused about what James is getting at.

However, suppose James had instead said:

> "I feel as a team we are getting a bit demotivated recently. I'd like to approach this in a bit of a different way *[or creative or innovative, whatever suits your team]* to see if we can get some discussions and ideas going.
>
> The situation reminds me of something that happened to me once."

Now the team knows what to expect, i.e. "something different", they also know their part in it is to "get some discussions and ideas going", and they know their Status in relation to James again, i.e., part of his team.

Beyond the opener, you can introduce storytelling to your team in familiar situations with familiar faces; this manages the SCARF elements of Certainty and Relatedness. Examples are listed in the box on the next page.

Now let's look more closely at the structure of a high impact story.

Team-building events
Informal meetings
Knowledge-sharing forums
Team away days
Review meetings
Mentoring sessions
Coaching sessions
Team development events

Structure of a story

We have already looked at deciding the AIMM and broad design of your stories in the *Preparing Stories* Chapter. According to Haven, "individual experiences only assume meaning within the context of a time-based, sequenced story" (2007: 35). A powerful and common story structure is the one that many film directors and playwrights use:

- Context (or every day events).
- Change or Conflict ("but then...").
- the Plot (explanation, interpretation, exploration).
- the Climax or Turning Point ("and then...").
- A Consequence ("and because of that...").
- And/or a Conclusion or Resolution ("and so...").

- Sometimes this is followed by a *Summary* or *Moral* of the story.
- Some stories also finish with a *Call to Action*.

Take a look at *The Wise Old Man and the Call Centre* in our stories section. The story begins with the context, the setting up of the call centres. Then comes the Conflict: *"But things did not work out well for the business managers."* The disappointing situation and loss of hope or dreams are explored as part of the Plot.

Then comes the Turning Point with the appearance of the old man. The second part of the story is the Resolution, implementing the wise old man's vision of rewarding and engaging with games and a faux Caribbean island and cocktails.

The story then ends with a succinct and relevant "Moral" relating the story back to the original context: *'When seeking to engage and motivate staff, study them at play.'* The concluding paragraph could also be seen as a Call to Action, i.e. this type of engagement could work with others.

Make the story message as clear as possible and you will not need to drive home the moral (this can sometimes be regarded as patronising and should be avoided).

The start (and end)

Perhaps it is the simplicity of stories that worries managers the most – that stories are "just for kids". The greatest fear may be the risk of seeming light-weight amongst colleagues, or even patronising. There is a risk of this – but we share insights throughout this book that will optimise your impact.

We have already shared a major tip we like to give managers and leaders at the start of this Chapter; don't introduce your story with "Let me tell you a story". In many cases, this is just too reminiscent of "Once Upon a Time" and can make people not used to storytelling in the workplace a bit uneasy.

Find another way to introduce your stories; some useful phrases are "that reminds me of something I heard recently..." or "I'd like to share something someone told me the other day..." or "A friend of mine once told me...".

After this, **get straight to the story**; there is no need to provide too much background detail although it is helpful to frame the story in a meaningful context. You'll find a great example of this in the tale *"The Whispering"*.

The storyteller gets us intrigued and into place and action with these opening lines:

> *"You don't want to do that now do you? It really wouldn't be a good idea would it?" There it was again, the Whispering voice from under the bed."*

This is also an example of **creating a "hook"**. Create something to gain the attention of the listener(s) at the beginning of your story that answer the questions: Why should I listen to this? What's in it for me? (the WIIFM).

The hook doesn't need to be elaborate, descriptive or shocking. Could you start your story with a simple introduction that tells me the WIIFM like the *"Brief Encounter* "story in this book?

It's also important to **select your first and last words and phrases carefully**; a tip from the literature is that the first paragraph should echo the last for impact.

Let's look at a simple example. In the first paragraph of *"Stone Soup"*, there is an old man travelling down the road towards the village; the last paragraph has him travelling down the road away from the village. This creates a satisfying self-contained structure to the story.

Let's take another example, *"Starfish"*. This has an evocative opening with the wild winter storm and a complete change of mood with the moral of "blowing sand up a dog's nose".

The first words set the scene, create a sense of danger and the last allow us to release our tension around the plight of the starfish and laugh. Humorous endings and morals can be very effective for embedding learning.

The middle

Once you have set up the story, remember the **Power of Three** as a device used in many folktales: three challenges, three magical strangers, three gifts; so consider repetition as a way of building your story.

Take a look at *"The Three Grains of Rice"*, using the power of three, the tale sets out the differing behaviour of the three princesses, so that we pay special attention to the third.

In *"The Little Devils and the Treasure"* the man is exhorted to look three times; it is the third time that he gets the realisation, and we are prepared to listen more closely by the teller using the Power of Three technique.

In the same way, **follow the "Goldilocks" principle**; not too much, not too little, but just the right amount of detail. Traditional tales like *"Stone Soup"* or *"Anansi"*, give sparse detail but it is enough.

And **consider the Point of View** (POV). Is the story more powerful and memorable narrated in the first person, for example, *"When I reached the village I found all the windows barred and shut..."* (see *"Stone Soup"*) or third person as this story is usually told?

Or look at *"Light My Fire"* – would this be more effective in the 3rd person, i.e. *"For Rob's 40th birthday, he was given a wonderful gift ..."*. There is no hard and fast rule other than what will engage your audience the most powerfully.

Or the POV could be from an unusual perspective, e.g. the story *"Starfish"* is told from the perspective of the starfish, so that we are much more aware of their plight and feelings. This is particularly useful to communicate without direct reference to people and therefore attacking aspects of SCARF.

Including **sensory information** in your story such as sights and sounds helps your listeners picture the context, "experience" it and identify with the story. *"Starfish"* is rich in sensory detail so that we can vividly see the beach, almost as if we were there.

And *"Light My Fire"* has the smell of smoke and sensory details such "acrid wisp", "coal black fragments" and "hot charred wood". Even a sparse traditional tale such as *"Stone Soup"* paints a picture with just enough details like "red tiled roofs", "curious silken purse" and "big iron cooking pot".

In the same way, use **potent images or metaphors** that condense and convey a great deal and resonate emotionally with your listeners, for example, "Stars and Stripes" doesn't just refer to a national flag, it holds the meaning of loyalty, shared history and values.

Similarly, "Men in Suits" is not about a fashion statement; it conveys hierarchy, power, and sometimes interference and disrespect.

What words or images does your organisation use to convey a great deal? Potent images allow the storyteller to be economic with images that have more "bang for their buck".

Think of the potency of the Holy Grail in *"The Leap of Faith"*. We don't need to be told that this a precious object worthy of brave pursuit. At another level, we understand the Grail at a more personal transformative level as a symbol of salvation.

We know this because of our culture; we may not have read the epic Mort d'Arthur with its quest for the Holy Grail but we will probably have seen one or more of the Indiana Jones' films. Your own business culture will have its own particular potent images, so listen out (and look out) for them.

We remember listening to one manager in a story skills workshop who was practising a "Who I Am" story. He began his tale with "I was driving my red Vauxhall Viva down the High Street". That red Vauxhall Viva was so perfectly chosen. His audience knew the era immediately (1970s) as well as his aspirations and possibly his income as a young man!

We once told the *"Stone Soup"* story at a Knowledge Management event. Afterwards we broke out into discussion groups: What could this story teach us? Was it relevant to our current issues? I was surprised to find that it was the "big iron cooking pot" that really captured the imagination of one group as a potent image.

For them, the pot symbolised community, and they elaborated on the metaphor, speculating what they could put into the pot.

Returning to the story telling techniques, the final point relates to the use of **pace and tone**. Use pauses in stories for effect and to let the message land. A slightly slower pacing of opening and closing phrases can work well, helping the listener process the information; in effect, you are respecting them as a listener.

A great storyteller of modern times is Barack Obama. His speeches are available on the internet. Listen out for the way he pauses and paces, as well as his use of potent images.

Key questions for now:

1. At the next formal presentation you attend:

    a. At what points could the speaker have told a story?

    b. What were the levels of engagement when a story <u>was</u> being told and when it <u>wasn't</u> – what was the difference?

    c. When was a story told that was not effective and got in the way of the points being made – why was this?

2. Spot when stories are being told in the media (TV, advertising, newspapers): what was the structure?

3. In your workplace:

    a. When and where are stories being told?

    b. How effective was the environment for the story listener? What kept the listeners' attention?

My key action points:

Now commit to three action points from this Chapter, by writing them here:

1.

2.

3.

References

Haven, K. (2007) *Story Proof – the Science Behind the Startling Power of Story*, Westport, CT: Libraries Unlimited.

Also see:

Simmons, A. (2007) *Whoever Tells the Best Story Wins*, New York: Amacom.

Sharing stories

Sharing stories:
overview and key points

In this Chapter we look at how sharing stories helps inspire a positive "towards state" beyond one-to-one interactions, and into the wider culture of organisations and the public space. We explore how stories can be co-created within a strategic framework, and offer some suggestions as to how managers can embed and implement story sharing in the workplace.

The key points of this Chapter are:

- The manager is not just a story "listener" and "teller"; they are also a story "harvester" and "curator".

- It is important to share stories in an environment of trust, and there are important ethical issues to consider when sharing stories.

- Finding ways of co-creating stories can be very empowering for teams as well as clients.

Stories as living organisms

The tale of *The Three Grains of Rice* beautifully illustrates how sharing stories can motivate a whole organisation to grow and prosper. Here's one interpretation of this classic Indian tale in relation to how people treat stories.

> The first daughter kept the grain of rice to herself not just in the palace but in a box; this leader or manager ignores others' development, preserves their status and operates in knowledge silos.
>
> The second daughter threw the grain of rice away; this leader or manager does not value stories, or trust them to motivate others.
>
> The third daughter however planted and nurtured her grain of rice; this leader or manager will share a powerful story or grain of knowledge, starting a process of organisational retelling to motivate others far beyond his or her own team.

However, stories are re-told across all levels of the organisation incorporating varying perspectives with each telling. Controlling the stories and their dissemination, and avoiding inaccurate or deliberately malicious re-interpretation can be perceived as a difficult issue for managers.

If stories are "released" into the work environment without being monitored as they spread, and if employees are also encouraged to share stories with impunity then this kind of storytelling culture can pose potential issues for managers used to a more traditionally controlled communication environment. As Reissner (2012: website) points out:

> Peer storytelling offers ways to make sense, to construct reality; however, this may be in conflict with the broader organizational direction and business requirement.

This is worth bearing in mind when using storytelling as a motivational tool, and managers must also consider the ethicality around sharing stories whether that be internally or in the public arena.

> **>Accept that stories have their own lives**

Ben Zander (2000), co-author of "The Art of Possibility" and conductor of the Boston Philharmonic Orchestra, notably recommends "upward spiral" conversations, those which inspire others.

So give your story a health check before airing it with your team – will it create an Upward Spiral? The acid test is to ask yourself:

> **>create stories that spin upward spirals of energy**

**"Whom does this serve?
Am I manipulating or motivating?"**

Having integrity

We call this having a sense of integrity in story work. There are two ways to optimise the integrity of stories once released into the organisation.

1) leaders and managers who tell tales must be seen to authentically "walk their talk"; any disparity between story and behaviour just breeds cynicism, poor motivation or even counter-stories.

2) a participative approach allows people to have ownership of the story telling process and pride in its integrity. Being "heard" is highly motivational whether one is a client or member of staff, and participating in the process of story sharing itself increases engagement and motivation.

One public service organisation we trained now has a team called the "Story Gatherers". Another client organisation has introduced "Inspiration Corner" as a regular agenda item to share stories that inspire and motivate.

So, other key questions to reflect on here are:

- When is a story "appropriate"?

- What are the boundaries in your workplace?

- What stories should you *not* tell?

- Who owns the story?

- How should it be stored to meet ethical and legal requirements?

Harvesting and curating

In addition to being a Story **Listener** and **Teller**, the role of the manager may also be that of Story **Harvester**, ensuring feedback mechanisms are created to capture stories from a multitude of voices, clients, partnership organisations, within and across teams.

A manager may also be a Story **Curator** ensuring that important stories are preserved not only to motivate, but also to educate, to share knowledge and convey values.

> **Being a story listener, teller, harvester and curator**

These stories can be shared on intranets, at community or partnership meetings, in staff newsletters, at conferences formally or in break-out groups. Wider platforms are public-facing websites, video or audio recordings, in leaflets and customer magazines, and in publications.

Such cross-fertilisation of shared stories is an opportunity to improve communication and encourage staff and client engagement at all levels. It is also an opportunity for innovation and improvement.

However when the only stories released into the public space are positive, yet staff on the ground are telling negative stories, this incongruity breeds cynicism and leads to worst case scenarios of neglect to address vital issues. High profile hospital failures in the UK have recently demonstrated this. The *Looking for Patterns* section in the *Listening to Stories* Chapter offers some useful principles here.

So learning from negative stories is another important part of story sharing. Rather like the *Who I Am* story which transforms failure into learning, negative stories can be a springboard to new shared learning and improvement.

Sharing these stories needs to be in a very inclusive and no-blame space, such as within a training setting, with a focus on learning together. Staff will also need to see that their embracing and transforming of a negative story really has influenced policy and practice, otherwise demoralisation is compounded.

In public service organisations, the motivation to use stories to influence policy development arises from the moral philosophy that the citizen or service user is at the centre of public services.

For example, teams involved with the *personalisation* of health and social care have a passion for allowing the client voice to be heard, and in our experience are motivated by the wider sharing of client stories and the potential for influencing decision making. (See Connect 4 Cymru, 2008).

In general, a useful practical technique for co-creating stories that then feed into an organisation's strategy and policy making is the SOAR process (Cooperrider, Kelley and Stavros, 2003).

SOAR, or "preferred future" planning, is a process that helps teams identify a future direction. It was developed by Appreciative Inquiry practitioners as a strategic tool. Rather than being focused on problem solving (or a 'liability' approach), it is asset-based, or focused on the strengths of a team or organisation.

But it is also inclusive and collaborative, as it uses open dialogue and inquiry to surface aspirations and dreams whilst emphasising personal ownership and action at all levels in the group – for Cooperrider and colleagues, these are key principles in achieving sustainable implementation.

SOAR is a creative and strategic process of strategic inquiry and appreciative intent:

Doing strategic inquiry into:

- Strengths: What are our greatest assets?

- Opportunities: What are the best opportunities in the organisation or marketplace?

Establishing appreciative intent:

- Aspirations: What is our preferred future (collectively agreed story)?

- Results: What are the measurable results we want? Who will be responsible?

We used SOAR with a training cohort of social workers and managers as a final review and evaluation exercise in their story skills training programme.

Using the model, we asked:

Strengths: What are our greatest assets (people, skills etc.)? What have we learnt, what skills have we acquired?

Opportunities: What are the best opportunities for us in our sector or organisation? What else is possible for us? What else is possible for our clients and service users? What else is possible for others?

Aspirations: What is my preferred future for this project? (Answered initially by individual team members of the project, followed by this second question...) What might our preferred future for this project be?

Results: What are the measurable results and outcomes we want for the project in the future?

Using this structure, we asked the cohort to break into two groups and complete the questions. We then asked them to tell their future story or appreciative intent, about what would be happening in 6 months, and how the project would look.

The cohort declared their intentions in the ways described in the box on the next page.

The participants crafted powerful preferred future stories, with measurable results and commitment to the project. These stories were told very positively to the plenary evaluation group; in part these stories motivated the forming of a support "board" to ensure the story project's sustainability.

1st Preferred Future

We will carry on developing our skills and understanding, and use this approach in all aspects of our personal and professional life. It is so important to use this experience and not to lose it. We are going to make sure that all the good things about the project don't get "bureaucratised". We want to see the stories flow out into all areas rather than being limited. We don't want our stories to have their "wings clipped".

2nd Preferred Future

As the first group of story gatherers in this project... We see ourselves pairing up and shadowing other professionals, for example social workers, or the Procurement Team, and with people from other private providers. Maybe we will pair up with the second cohort of gatherers in the next project. We have learnt so much through sharing and networking and would like this to continue and be taken forward. Not get lost!

We provide a some blank SOAR questions on the next few pages to help guide you in your own SOAR activity.

SOAR Tool

Strengths: What are our greatest assets?

Opportunities: What are the best opportunities in the organisation or marketplace?

Aspirations: What is our preferred future (collectively agreed story)?

Results: What are the measurable results we want? Who will be responsible?

SOAR Tool

Strengths: What are our greatest assets?

Opportunities: What are the best opportunities in the organisation or marketplace?

Aspirations: What is our preferred future (collectively agreed story)?

Results: What are the measurable results we want? Who will be responsible?

SOAR Tool

Strengths: What are our greatest assets?

Opportunities: What are the best opportunities in the organisation or marketplace?

Aspirations: What is our preferred future (collectively agreed story)?

Results: What are the measurable results we want? Who will be responsible?

Recapping on what we have learnt about sharing stories so far, we find that sharing stories is not a top-down process nor dependent on formal occasions. Allowing teams to share "Future Stories" can be motivating and help to redress any imbalance in the team or more widely within the organisation.

Sharing stories can also help with knowledge sharing within teams. The table below views sharing stories in the context of the SCARF model and illustrates how story sharing can encourage team cohesion, innovation, best practice and motivation for high performance.

Status
Integrating story sharing as a regular team practice allows people to explore what is important to the team and reaffirm individual relationships within the team in a safe way.

Certainty
Story sharing, particularly of motivating Future Stories, gives people an opportunity to define the future for themselves. Sharing and developing these stories can contribute to best practice in an innovative way.

Autonomy

Introducing ways of sharing team stories is a meaningful way to feed into decision making, and helps individual team members feel they are able to shape and influence policy and direction.

Relatedness

Story sharing engenders an environment of trust between team members, or as Forbes columnist Terrence Gargiulo has said, *"The shortest distance between two people is a story."*

Fairness

Having one's story shared and heard helps redress any feeling of unfairness. Sharing stories may also encourage compassion for others and empathy.

There is a lot to be learnt in sharing stories for an Upward Spiral. We have seen the significant transformations stories can make when used for wider social good rather than personal gain.

We invite you to read and re-read this book as many times as you need to get insight – use it, write in it, scribble in it, or whatever you need to do that helps you.

Use notes to capture your learning and remind you on a daily basis – like we have throughout this book:

For now, we would like to share a last thought for now, from the British writer, Philip Pullman:

After nourishment,
shelter and companionship,
stories are the thing
we need most in the world.

So, how are you satisfying these needs with your team?

Key questions for now:

1. When do I "walk the talk"?

2. When do I NOT "walk the talk"?

3. What are the key story sharing methods already operating in my organisation? How could I use them?

4. How could I retell *The Three Grains of Rice* story as a motivational exercise, perhaps in a more modern idiom?

5. What ethical issues do I need to address before sharing a story? Would a story ethics charter be helpful?

6. What client stories are there already being shared that could be used as a springboard for new learning and service improvements?

My key action points:

Now commit to three action points from this Chapter, by writing them here:

1.

2.

3.

References

Connect 4 Cymru (2008) *The Use of Citizens Stories in Policy Development:* http://www.wales.nhs.uk/sitesplus/829/opendoc/117004.

Cooperrider, D.L., Kelley, D.L., Stavros, J.M. (2003) Strategic Inquiry > Appreciative Intent: Inspiration to SOAR: A New Framework for Strategic Planning: AI Practitioner, *International Journal of Appreciative Inquiry,* Nov 2003.

Keller S. & Price C. (2010) *Performance and Health: An evidence-based approach to transforming your organisation,* McKinsey and Company.

Reissner, S. and Pagan, V. (2012) *Manifestations of storytelling in management practice:* http://www.managerial-storytelling.com/.

Zander, B. & Zander, R. (2000) *The Art of Possibility: Transforming Professional and Personal Life,* Cambridge, MA: Harvard Business School Press.

Stories for motivation

A Personal Philosophy of Facilitation

Bob Meakin

In my view, the art of facilitation is best exemplified by considering the Master Carpenter guiding Apprentices on their journey to craftsmanship. The Master will seek to inform, to demonstrate, to criticise well and to praise more – but, most of all, to inspire.

The first lesson may well be the consideration of examples of the Master's work, not as a celebration of achievement, but rather as a source of inspiration. The first message will be, 'This is the like of which we shall achieve together. From this point on, there is no limit for you.'

The journey will begin swiftly and engage all the senses: the singing of the saw, the smoothness of finely finished timber, the glint on the edge of the keenest chisel, the heady smell of varnish.

No one shall finish this journey without suffering the odd blackened fingernail, a cut or two, and a small forest of splinters, but long-term strength shall grow out of short-term adversity.

The length of the journey is known and much of its detail planned. A range of skills is listed, but the time allocated to each is not fixed. There will follow a programme of both macro- and micro-lessons, each carefully planned to build upon the knowledge and skills imparted during the last, and each forming a significant loop in an upward spiral.

Many skills will be revisited, each time with an added degree of challenge. The plan shall also remain flexible enough to embrace timely opportunities for unplanned learning which will be seen as a valuable addition to the programme rather than a distraction from it.

The Master will instil confidence that the greatest benefit will be gained through mastery of the process, rather than the completion of any specific project. A keen knowledge of the best materials to work with and the best tools for each task will form a sound foundation for that process.

The Apprentice will learn that 90% of his work can be achieved through the efficient use of only 5% of the toolbox. However, it will be in his mastering of the rest that will distinguish his work. He will learn that the cutting of fine detail upon a piece with unstable legs will prove of little lasting value.

Not all Apprentices will achieve the level of knowledge and skill of their Master, yet some will exceed it; the good Master will appreciate the achievement of all. He will identify strengths among weaknesses and be prepared to guide each student according to individual needs.

Moreover, he will be open to the challenges brought by the possessor of greater potential skill than his own, welcoming the chance to give wings to that talent. He may feel uneasy should an Apprentice find an established method unsound, or a faithful tool unsatisfactory; he will nonetheless encourage perceptive criticism that may lead to the evolution of a new method, even the design of a superior tool, all to the greater good of the Guild.

For what greater honour is there for a Master Carpenter than to be an inspiration for a great Cabinet Maker?

Some reflective questions:

- What does the story tell us about how we can motivate someone to achieve their potential?

- What might need to change in your work to help motivate people in these ways?

- In what ways is this similar to how you facilitate performance in others?

- In what ways is this different to how you facilitate performance in others?

- What might you do differently as a result?

Anansi the Spider, Part 1: Anansi and his Six Sons

A traditional West African story retold by Lisa Rossetti

Anansi the Spider had six sons, and each of his sons had a special talent.

Anansi's first son was called "Trouble Seer," and he could see any kind of trouble from far far away.

The second son, called "Road Builder," could build roads through any kind of terrain.

The third son, named "River Drinker," could make rivers become dry, with not a drop of water in them.

The fourth son was "Animal Skinner," and he was very good at removing the skins from animals.

Fifth was "Rock Thrower," who could throw rocks for great distances and with complete accuracy.

And the sixth son was "Ground Pillow," who could lie on the ground and make it soft, so soft.

One day, Anansi left his home to travel far and wide. He was gone one week, then two weeks, then three weeks, until at last more than a month had gone by, and his sons grew worried.

Trouble Seer, Anansi's first son, looked far and wide. "Do you see our father? Do you see him?" asked all his brothers. "Yes," said Trouble Seer. "He has fallen into a river on the other side of the dark, dense, dangerous jungle."

Upon hearing that, Road Builder, the second son, immediately built a road through the dark, deep, dangerous jungle, and the six brothers travelled along the road until they came to a wide, raging river.

River Drinker, the third son, drank and drank and drank until the wide, raging river ran dry. There in the middle of the river lay a huge fish, and they could hear Anansi calling for help from inside the fish. Animal Skinner, the fourth son, quickly cut the fish open and released Anansi.

But a huge eagle was hovering overhead watching and waiting, and as soon as Anansi emerged free from the fish, the eagle swooped down and grabbed him with its sharp talons, and flew off high into the sky.

When Rock Thrower, the fifth son, saw this he grabbed a rock from the bottom of the dried-up river and threw it at the eagle, hitting the bird with such perfect accuracy that it immediately dropped Anansi, who dropped like a stone towards the earth from a vast height.

But Ground Pillow, the sixth and last son, lay on the ground directly beneath him as his father plummeted to earth. Ground Pillow made the earth soft, so soft, so that when Anansi finally hit the ground, he was completely unhurt. And so it was that the six brothers saved their father, Anansi the Spider.

Some reflective questions:

- What brought the sons together?

- What brings your team together?

- What did the sons do to be a great team in a crisis?

- How does this story relate to a recent example of great teamwork in your organisation? What was the motivating factor for success? Other than a crisis, what motivates your team?

- What would you call the special talents that you bring to your team? Be imaginative! (e.g. someone with IT skills could call themselves "Web Weaver"; someone who is good with people could call themself "Heart Toucher").

- What would you call the special talents that each team member brings to the team?

Anansi the Spider,
Part 2: Anansi and the Moon

A traditional West African story retold by Lisa Rossetti

Now Anansi decided to reward his six sons for saving him from the fish and for their bravery and efforts. But what could he give them? The next day, he went walking in the forest, and there he saw a curious sight.

Deep in the forest hidden amongst the trees, a beautiful, round object hovered, glowing softly. This object was called Moon, and Anansi picked it up and brought it home. "Oh, what a wonderful prize this is," he said, "to give to one of my sons for saving my life!"

Anansi called his six sons. "See what I have found," said Anansi, "This is a reward for saving my life." His six sons looked at Moon and each of them wanted to have Moon for his very own.

Each of them thought, "If I have the Moon, then my hut will be brightly lit and beautiful and all the people in the village will admire and respect me."

Trouble Seer said, "The prize should be mine, for if I had not seen my father, we could not have saved him."

Road Builder said, "No, it's mine, for if I had not built the road through the jungle, we could not have gotten to my father in time."

River Drinker said, "But for if I had not emptied the river, we could not have gotten to my father to save him."

Animal Skinner said, "That's not fair, for if I had not cut open the big fish, my father would have remained within it."

Rock Thrower said, "You must give it to me, for if I had not thrown the rock at the eagle, it would have flown off with my father."

Ground Pillow said, "You're wrong, for if I had not made the ground soft, so soft, my father would have died when he hit the ground."

They argued and squabbled for days and days and days on end, until at last Anansi got sick of listening to them. So he called on Nyame, the God of All Gods, to come down to earth to help him.

Anansi gave the Moon to Nyame, and asked Nyame to give it to whichever of the six sons deserved it most. But Nyame couldn't decide and grew tired of their arguing and bickering.

Then Trouble Seer paused from his bickering. He sensed something was wrong. He looked up and saw that Nyame was angry. The six brothers stopped their fighting for a moment but they still couldn't agree who should be the winner.

Anansi didn't know what to do next. So Nyame, God of All Gods, went to his wife and said "Wife, what can we do? Who should get the reward?"

But his wife said "Oh that's easy! This is what you do." And she whispered in her husband's ear. At first Nyame wasn't sure. But his wife said "Trust me." So Nyame went to Anansi and whispered in his ear. Anansi saw the wisdom of it and agreed.

And so Anansi went back to his sons and said "Listen to me. I wanted to reward one of you but I was wrong. So listen to what I'm going to say." And the six sons finally stopped fighting and listened to their father. And so it was that they understood the wisdom of Nyame's wife, and they nodded humbly.

So Anansi handed Nyame (God of All Gods) the Moon. Nyame went back up into his sky home carrying the bright, softly glowing Moon up into the sky with him. And there the Moon has remained to this very day. It shines its light on everyone's hut in every village in the whole world, bringing hope and clarity to the darkest night.

Some reflective questions:

- The six brothers first responded to a crisis in a united way. What caused them to fall out? What brought them back together?

- What reward systems do you have in your organisation? Are they fair? Do they effectively acknowledge collective effort and motivate your teams?

- How could this story help you with a team issue or motivational challenge you are facing at the moment?

- How might your reward system in your own workplace connect or contrast with this story?

- What other options might there be to reward or acknowledge people in your workplace?

Brief Encounter:
The Power of Happy Accidents

Peter Cook

I meet lots of people who want to achieve great things but who don't always know how to nurture their own inner motivation to do whatever it takes, especially in relation to the dreaded sphere of networking. This story tells us that success depends both on planning and the ability to capitalise on happy accidents.

My story starts at the Open University Business School, who had asked me to make a film to help them market the business school to prospective students.

The resulting film "Punk Rock Business" drew acclaim from their key academics and resulted in an invite to their inaugural professorial lecture by Evan Davis, Presenter of BBC Radio 4's Today Programme and BBC One's Dragons Den.

I was keen to present Evan with copies of my books but how would I do this? There would be more than 200 people present and no time to explain my reasons for wanting to connect.

The answer that arrived to my problem came quite by chance.

I arrived at Milton Keynes train station to find Evan on the platform, looking for the stairs. I asked:

> "Are you going to the Open University Evan?"

He froze. I suspect he thought he was being approached by a busker, as I was wearing a suit over a Sex Pistols t-shirt with a burnt guitar slung over my shoulder!

Once he realised I was a University tutor, business consultant and rock musician and not a stalker, he kindly invited me to share a taxi to the University, which he paid for. What a gentleman!

It turned out that Evan wanted to know more about the type of audience he would be facing, so I was able to help him tune into the event.

We then moved on to more general discussions about economics and what I did at the University and outside. Evan kindly accepted the copies of the books and agreed to have a read in between everything else he does. I seriously doubt I would have achieved the same result in the hustle and bustle of a busy event.

This chance opportunity for a 1:1 conversation proved vital to me subsequently in conversations with Bloomberg TV, The BBC, The Independent, The Guardian and members of The Bank of England's Monetary Policy Committee, when I released a rock song about economics called "Fiscal Cliff".

I subsequently appeared on BBC Radio 4 although I am unsure if this was directly related to my brief encounter with Evan. What then are the lessons from this story?

Lesson # 1. Successful networking relies on prepared spontaneity

Lesson # 2. Remain open and receptive to the unexpected

Postscript: I seem to be somewhat accident prone, having almost literally bumped into Evan in his running gear 9 months later at Earls Court tube station.

What you do with life's accidents is not an accident however ...

Some reflective questions:

- In what ways was Peter open and receptive to the unexpected?

- In what ways was Peter prepared for spontaneity?

- How did these things help motivate Evan?

- What things could you do in your team to help motivate in such a way?

Get Back On That Horse

Heather Meakin

I started horse riding at the age of four, and still love it just as much now even though I'm a grown up fifteen year old. But it hasn't been a perfect eleven years. When I was almost seven, my riding instructor at the time gave me a new horse to ride in my lessons. Usually, I rode one of three horses, but today was different. Today I rode Strawberry, a beautiful mare, who had recently arrived at the stables from a busy, eventing lifestyle. The world she had just entered was a much calmer one where the riders often had little experience. Being a confident rider, and one who is perfectly happy to try new things, I mounted Strawberry with a smile on my face and a familiar glow in my heart.

The lesson began normally - walking, trotting and cantering exercises were first. It was then time for jumping. After watching two other girls complete the course with ease, I volunteered to go next. Strawberry responded well to my commands, gently trotting in a 20m circle before heading for the jumps.

All was going as planned, my horse was collected and I rode her positively towards the first fence. Excitement fluttered in my stomach as we both prepared ourselves for the brief flight. Nothing could go wrong.

Strawberry began to take off, so I folded into my jump position. I arched forwards, hunched over her neck and aiming straight ahead.

Suddenly, the ground was rushing to meet me. At the very last second, Strawberry had swerved to the side, away from the obstacle whilst I continued to rocket ahead. Within seconds I crashed downwards, straight onto the jump. Excruciating pain shot through my arm and I realised that I'd awkwardly landed on it. In a daze, and shocked at the event, I attempted to move my injured limb and found that as much as I tried I could not. I began to scream out loud.

Blinded by tears due to pain and humiliation, I curled into a ball as if I was trying to hide from the world. I listened to my heart, loudly beating in my ears and over it I could hear little else. I picked out my Dad's voice as he rushed to my side and also the voice of a child who claimed Strawberry would have cleared the jump if she had been riding. Embarrassed and suffering from unbearable pain, I remember being rushed home and then into hospital for an x-ray.

My arm was not broken, but was dislocated at the shoulder and I was unable to lift it high above my head. No matter how much my parents attempted to reassure me, I was convinced that the fall was my fault and that I was not a good rider.

"Think about last year's gymkhana!", my Mum said to me. "You came 1st, 2nd and 3rd in three different events!" But the memory failed to brighten my mood. Horrible thoughts such as 'I can't do it,' 'I made a fool of myself,' 'I'm not good enough' began to eat away at my confidence until I finally made the decision that I wouldn't ride again.

I don't know what changed my mind six months later. My arm had healed and I was determined to get back into the saddle. I suppose I missed the warm feeling I experienced when involved with horses. But also, I often lay in bed at night remembering how strong I felt when riding. I didn't get that feeling during any other activity and I was sure I couldn't live without it. That sense of confidence was missing.

My parents found me a new riding school. Somewhere I would be pushed to improve my skills. I would learn new things to advance my riding and to help me handle a situation, like the one with Strawberry, differently, and come out of it firmly still in the saddle on my horse.

It's hard not to give up when you are knocked down. It's particularly difficult to do so if you are not confident within an activity. However, making mistakes and experiencing unfortunate incidents will help you to learn how to avoid them next time. In the process you will gain back your confidence and may even be taught something new which could help you to improve your skills and knowledge.

If you fall - get back on that horse.

Some reflective questions:

- What are the key things that motivated the horse rider to carry on regardless of the trauma?

- What have been the setbacks for your team in the past?

- What have been the obstacles for your team in the past?

- What have these obstacles or setbacks stopped your team from doing?

- What might be worth trying again?

iBusy

Tony Wall

I am active 100% of the time. And my battery is like a yo-yo; up and down all day.

I awaken with my battery at 100%. I start to feed on the constant stream of emails as I hear the gurgle of mouth wash being consumed in the bathroom.

I answer the first 100 emails with lightning speed. I hardly notice I've done it; I'm so efficient. The digital 'swoosh' sound fills me with intense pleasure and satisfaction that I have answered a question or solved a problem.

By the time we get to the office I am hot; I've already earned my keep.

I am on my toes every second. My battery is taking a beating.

By midday, I need my juice. I am at 20%. We are anxious that my battery is dying. I could shut off at any second.

We seek out sockets; looking round corners, looking under tables, asking everyone we see where the nearest socket is.

By the time we find a socket, I'm desperate; I'm chugging along like a steam engine. I'm no longer high performance. No longer shiny, but sweating like a pig.

I take slow sips of juice. I rejuvenate, slowly. Very slowly.

As I rest on the desk, I slow down. I see life from a different angle. I see the flowers on the desk. I smell them. I feel the breeze from the window on my side. Ever so slight. But I feel it.

I see the smiles and cheeky winks that my colleagues throw at each other. I see playfulness. I see happiness. I am still getting the emails, but I feel different things in them. I sense anxiety of the senders; one word answers do not satisfy their thirst for information. I sense gratitude in others; when problems have been solved. I feel alive.

The race starts again when I hit 70%; enough to meet the torment of the email life...

By night, I hit 1%.

I'm tired again. I'm so very tired.

I use that 1% to remind myself of the flowers on the desk. The breeze. The smiles and cheeky winks. I reminisce of that beautiful state where I can enjoy small moments in my hectic life. Small moments, but powerfully uplifting and energising.

As I appreciate my life, I drift and finally allow myself to shut off. I drift into 0%.

Some reflective questions:

- Is this talking about the smart phone or the professional? Which do you relate to more?

- What are your battery levels right now? What are your battery levels throughout the day?

- What do you do to maintain your energies throughout the day?

- In which moments throughout your day are you *really* paying attention to the events and people around you?

- What could you do balance energies through the day, in terms of:

  o Your own working practices?

  o Team working practices?

  o Work flow processes or policies?

Light My Fire

Rob Jones

For my 40th birthday, I was given a wonderful gift; a week-long Bushcraft course at Ray Mear's Woodlore School. The first part of the course was instruction and practice in a wide range of survival skills, leading up to a formal assessment on the final day. I quickly mastered building shelters and foraging for food, but as hard I tried I could not make fire by friction to warm my shelter or cook my food.

The final day came all too quickly. I was able to easily demonstrate making cordage and tools from natural materials, and how to navigate by the sun, stars or natural features, but I knew I was putting off the inevitable, and the one skill which would keep me at a pass rather than a merit or distinction. At this point I was exhausted from the lack of sleep, weak from lack of food and filthy from lack of water to wash in.

Somehow, I summoned the energy to once again take up the bow I'd crafted from a curved rhododendron branch, wrap the string around the drill, and place it between the wooden blocks with a few fresh leaves to act as lubrication at the top.

Once again, I pushed my weight down on the drill to hold it in place, and began the task of pulling the bow backwards and forwards to spin the drill.

For long minutes there was nothing. Then, as the muscles in my back, arms and legs started to complain, I could smell the faint aroma of smoke, followed by a miniscule wisp from the point where the drill rubbed against the hollow of my block. I'd been here so many times before, only to collapse when my body could take no more, and never achieving more than an acrid wisp.

However, this time was different. I was being observed, and Willow, the Instructor (yes, that was her real name!) stood by with words of encouragement. As the aches became agony, the cuts and blisters on my hands adding to the torment, I could see the wisp grow, and soon tiny coal black fragments were gathering in the notch.

After an eternity, I had a pea-sized clump of hot charred wood. Would it be enough to fan into flame? I carefully tipped it into my prepared dry tinder, and drew the bundle to my lips. The gentlest breath revealed a faint glow, to be followed by further breaths, until the ember shone like a tiny sun, and then caught on the dry bracken. That first flame was nurtured with as much care as a newborn, but it grew quickly and soon became a blaze.

Despite the pain, in that one moment I felt more alive than I ever had, more proud and more connected to my past. I had achieved more than I thought possible, thanks to the encouragement of another person. I, a 21st century Human Resources Manager, hands soft through years of office work, felt connected to my prehistoric ancestors. I burst into a grin that would last for weeks.

Some reflective questions:

- How important is it to be linked to our past (or ancestors) to motivate us?

- How could you use this story to motivate your team or an individual?

- Who has encouraged you in your life to make that extra effort?

- Who might you encourage?

- Effort doesn't have to be superhuman to be successful; in Rob's story it was the "gentlest breath" that produced fire. How can you relate this to your challenges?

Stone Soup

A traditional tale from Eastern Europe retold by Lisa Rossetti

In a far-off land, an old stranger was making a journey. He had a stout stick in his hand, a cloak over his shoulders, and at his belt he carried a curious silken purse. And so he travelled for miles far and wide, up hill and down dale, when he saw in the distance a small village hidden deep in the valley. He could see the red tiled roofs and fields but strangely he could see no smoke rising from the chimneys.

Still he made his way towards the village down a winding path. As he entered the village square, the villagers retreated into their homes, locking their doors and closing their wooden shutters. For there had been generations of war and poor harvests, and they were afraid of strangers. But one little child hid behind the corner of her house and peeked out at him. Her mother came out of her cottage to pull her child indoors out of harm's way. As she hesitated in her doorway the stranger walked closer.

The stranger smiled and asked, "Why are you all so frightened. I am just a simple traveller, looking for a safe place to stay for the night and a warm meal."

"There's not a bite to eat in the whole province," said the woman. "We are weak and our children are starving. Better keep moving on."

"Oh, I have everything I need," he said. "In fact, I was thinking of making some stone soup to share with all of you."

He asked the woman to fetch a big iron cooking pot from her kitchen. Then he asked her husband to fill it with water. Next he asked their neighbour to bring sticks and build a fire under it. Then, with great ceremony, he drew an ordinary-looking stone from his curious silken purse and dropped it into the simmering cooking pot.

By now, hearing the rumour of food, some of the villagers were beginning to peek from behind their shutters. Gradually they ventured out of their homes and gathered around the steaming cooking pot. As the stranger sniffed the "broth" and licked his lips in anticipation, hunger began to overcome their fear.

"Ahh," the stranger said to himself rather loudly, "I do like a tasty stone soup. But stone soup with a little bit of cabbage – now that's hard to beat."

Soon a villager approached hesitantly, holding a small cabbage he'd retrieved from its hiding place in the thatch, and added it to the pot. "Wonderful!!" cried the stranger.

"You know, I once had stone soup with cabbage and a bit of salt beef as well, and it was fit for a king." By now the pot was beginning to give off a delicious fragrance enticing the whole village to gather round.

The village butcher managed to find some salt beef that he'd hidden away in his cellar for hard times... and so it went on. Soon potatoes, onions, carrots, mushrooms, beans were added to the pot, until there was indeed a delicious meal for everyone in the village to share. And so all the village and all the children finally went to bed with full stomachs and smiles on their faces.

In the morning, the stranger picked up his staff, threw his cloak over his shoulders and fastened the silk purse to his belt. He took his leave waving goodbye to the children who came giggling and laughing out of the cottages. But the village elders soon stopped him at the crossroads at the edge of town.

The villager elders offered the stranger a great deal of money for his "magic" stone, but he refused to sell it.

They persisted, offering him even more money. Then he said, "Think about it. What was the real magic of the stone?"

.

Then the village elders thought deeply. They thought about the little child who had first been so curious about the stranger. They thought about the cooking pot and the fire. They thought about the first gift of cabbage and salt beef.

And finally they nodded and smiled. They had understood. And so the old stranger left them and walked on down the winding path to the next village, carrying his stone with him in its curious silken purse.

Some reflective questions:

- Who or what is your "village"?

- What are you hiding from the rest of your village? (e.g. strengths, talents, resources, knowledge, connections).

- What is the smallest but most powerful thing you can offer (your "Magic Stone")?

- When will you use it? With whom? Who else could you use it with?

The Leap of Faith

Vicky Evans

Indiana Jones stands on a narrow ledge. Inches from his toes is a massive drop to rocks below and a chasm extends 100 feet across to be met by another cliff wall. On the other side of that chasm lies the Holy Grail. He is shaking and sweating. He can see no way across.

> *You* may not be standing on the edge of a cliff, but given the way you feel – you might as well be. You have an idea – something that you'd just love to do. You keep thinking about it but you feel stuck because it looks impossible. You can't see how you can get from where you are now to where you want to be.

"Indy... Indy, you must hurry!!"

His friend Brody reminds him how important it is for him to find the Holy Grail. He has spent the whole film – "Indiana Jones and the Last Crusade" – looking for it. The stakes are high: his father will die if he doesn't find it. It's too important not to try something.

Lives may not depend on *your* idea. It may even look safer for everybody if you don't do it. But, if this idea is something that you feel passionate about, if it feels exciting and somehow right for you, then, in a way, your life does depend on it. And, when you think about it, you know that.

Indiana hears his father shout:

"You must believe, boy, you must... believe."

Indiana Jones takes a deep breath. Then he does it. He steps out into space. He is in mid-air. He's not going to make it. His hands reach for the opposite wall but he is going to fall to his death. And then – he doesn't! He lands on his hands and knees and somehow he's held up by thin air.

How did he not fall? He looks down and suddenly he can see that he is standing on a carved stone bridge across the gap. He couldn't see it before because it blended into the pattern of the brown cliff on the other side. It was a marvellous illusion. There *is* a way across. He just couldn't see it from the ledge. He had to take a step to find it. That one step has changed what he can see. Now he can see the next steps he needs to take.

Whatever *you* want to do, take one step. You may not be able to see what steps, if any, might follow that first one. Taking even one action is powerful and changes what you can see as possible. It also changes how you feel about yourself because then you know that you are someone who can take a step even when you are stuck and afraid. You've just shown yourself how bold you can be.

You have an idea – something that you'd just love to do but you feel stuck because it looks impossible. Take lessons from Indiana Jones and take that one step. It's the most powerful thing you can do. And you don't even need to wear a swashbuckling hat – unless you want to, of course.

Some reflective questions:

- What makes your idea important to you? What excites you about this idea?

- Who encourages you? Who could you ask to support you?

- What small step could you take towards your 'Holy Grail'? When will you take this step?

The Little Devils and the Treasure

Vicky Evans

There was once a man who was becoming more unhappy as each year went by. All his life he had heard stories about a wonderful treasure in a country far away. One day he decided that he wanted a different life and he set off to seek the treasure. As he walked along, he noticed an angel on his shoulder, whispering quietly:

"Keep going. This is important."

He wasn't sure when it landed there; perhaps the angel had been there all along.

As the border of the far away country came into view, the adventurer could see beyond it to some hills which were lit with a beautiful glow. The stories were true! The treasure was there! The adventurer's heart started to glow too. He was striding out strongly now, eager to reach the place where the treasure glowed so beautifully.

Soon he passed by a stone wall where two people were sitting, chatting in the sunshine. They shouted out to him and asked him where he was going. When he told them about the treasure, they nodded sagely to each other, shook their heads and started to tell him about all the pitfalls on the journey, how they had seen so many people try and fail.

"It's so difficult. It can't be done. Are you sure you really want to do this? Have you got what it takes? Aren't you worried you might fail?"

He could see they had a point: they were only telling him what he had been thinking anyway. Soon his head seemed to be full of voices telling him this was a stupid adventure and he should know better. In the end it all seemed too much and he ran back to his home as fast as possible.

However, he wasn't happy when he was back at home. He just couldn't forget the glow of the treasure. Occasionally he even heard the angel on his shoulder whispering about going to have another search for it. Eventually he set out again.

After he had travelled a little way, he heard a noise behind him on the path. He turned and saw a friend from his village hurrying towards him: his family needed him urgently. He must hurry back to care for them.

"Now isn't the time to do what you want to do. How can you even think of it? How can you be so selfish?"

And so, with a heavy heart, the adventurer returned home for a second time.

Some time later, he set out for the treasure again. He got further than he had before and came to a huge forest. There was no way round it. He had to go through it. He took a deep breath and plunged into it. At first he seemed to make good progress but then he started to doubt himself. Hadn't he seen this group of trees before?

"You don't know what you're doing. This is madness - you need to know the way before you do something like this."

Soon he was stumbling around, hopelessly lost. It was too much: he felt like curling up in a ball and hoping it was all a bad dream. To make matters worse, it was getting dark and now there seemed to be dangers lurking behind every tree.

Suddenly a twig cracked and he jumped.

"This isn't safe. I've got to get out of here!"

He turned and ran, tripping over tree roots and getting scratched by thorns in his desperation to get away.

But the adventurer didn't want to abandon the treasure so he just kept moving backwards and forwards: not returning home but not crossing over the frontier into the land where the treasure lay. He felt frustrated with the unfairness of it all.

Eventually, exhausted, the adventurer sat down and put his head in his hands. "What's going on?" he sobbed. "Why can't I get across the frontier?" The answer came as the faintest whisper:

"Look and you will see".

He raised his head and looked around, but he saw nothing at all. He put his head back in his hands.

"Look a second time."

He looked up again. To his amazement he saw that he was surrounded by small devilish creatures. One of them was running around him in circles. Another was perching on his shoulder, chattering loudly in his ear, while a couple were tugging on his clothes, pulling him towards home. In different ways, these little devils were all working hard to keep him from the treasure.

Now that he could see them, the adventurer found that he had more options: he worked out how to get closer to the frontier by dodging around them or ignoring them and doing it anyway. These tactics worked for a while and he got much closer to the frontier than ever before. But it was hard work: just as he found one tactic that worked, his little devils would invent a new trick to trip him up. However hard he tried, he still couldn't get to the treasure. In frustration, he stopped again. "What can I do?"

"Look into their eyes."

He looked into the eyes of the little devil nearest to him and to his surprise he saw a little child, afraid and desperate to be safe. He was filled with compassion for that child and he knew what he had to do.

"It's OK now" and he bent to pick the child up and placed it on his shoulder where it promptly yawned and fell asleep.

One by one, he looked into the eyes of his little devils and picked them up. When he had them all, he walked calmly over the frontier and towards the treasure as the children slept.

Some reflective questions:

- What is "the treasure" for you?

- When you start to move towards what you really want to do, what happens? What patterns or "little devils" can you spot?

- As you notice your "little devil" patterns, what options do you have?

- To what extent can you feel compassion for your own "little devils" and their attempts to keep you safe?

The Mule and the Jelly Fish

Tony Wall

The Mule worked at a beautiful sun-drenched beach with pale sands, blue waters and a constantly flowing, cool breeze. He'd worked there for years; he loved his job.

The Mule loved taking the same route around a small section of the beach day in, day out, year after year. He'd usually be transporting a small child on his back. He still couldn't understand why, after so many years, people would pay to put their child on his back. But he loved it.

He knew what he needed to do and when he needed to do it. He knew what the sandy path under his hooves would entail, and felt confident in each stride that the journey would be safe.

One day, on his usual round, The Mule noticed the sea creeping unusually close to his well trodden path. He became worried. It stretched closer and closer until the edge of the sea had touched his front left hoof.

He didn't know what was happening. He didn't know what to do. He stopped. He was still. He could feel his heart pounding with anxiety.

As he stood there, paralysed with fear, he noticed an unusual shape, not too far away from him, drifting in the water towards him.

The shape seemed to flow with the gentle waves and motions of the sea, following the movements effortlessly, almost without a concern or worry in the world. It didn't ride the waves; it danced eloquently with the waves.

The Mule said to the shape: "What are you and how do you do it?"

"I'm a Jelly Fish and how do I do what?" the shape replied.

The Mule continued: "You make it look so easy to go with the flow!"

The Jelly Fish reflected and said: "Ah, well, in my line of work it's good to be able to be fluid and flex - it makes it so easy to move when the tides change. And the tides change pretty much every second for me!".

"I see" said The Mule. "But how can you know your path or where you'll end up?"

As The Jelly Fish drifted off into a different direction, she asked "You know, Mule, what is the worst that could happen if you let go of having to know either your path or your destination? What would happen if you just enjoyed the dance of your life?"

The Mule's initial reaction was that the Jelly Fish was a fool. But over time, The Mule reflected long and hard. He came to admire the Jelly Fish. She was open and responsive to the tides she found herself in. She was open to the new experiences offered to her by her journey, including talking to a Mule! But he could not become a Jelly Fish; he was a Mule, and a happy one at that.

Years later, The Mule was happily at work on the beach. Transporting a child eating an ice cream melting in the summery sun. It wasn't the same path, though. The Mule had varied his route ever so slightly over the years; he enjoyed the new experiences this slight meandering could offer.

His attention was quickly drawn to the sandy beach floor - the child had accidently dropped his ice cream onto the ground.

The Mule was tempted by this opportunity for a very tasty sweet treat, but his attention quickly zoomed elsewhere.

He realised that he had been traipsing through a shallow sea drift. And he wasn't fazed or anxious. Far from it; he was enjoying the cool splashes of water against his strong worn legs.

And at that moment, he realised he had become, in his very own little way, that Jelly Fish he had come to admire.

Some reflective questions:

- How else could The Mule be like the Jelly Fish?

- What were the strengths of The Mule's approach to his work?

- What were the implications of it?

- What were the strengths of the Jelly Fish's approach?

- What were the implications of it?

- What might we gain if we became more like The Mule or the Jelly Fish?

- What might we lose if we became more like The Mule or the Jelly Fish?

The Starfish
– an end to apathy!

A tale re-told by Lizzie Gates

The winter sea rolled in, throwing waves as high as houses across the shore. And, when at last the storm was over, hundreds of starfish found themselves scattered and vulnerable, awaiting death. The night was filled with their silent screams and their despair.

As the sun returned, its warmth soothed them. But they knew that, as the sun rose, the pleasant warmth they now felt would turn to pain. They would be parched. And they would long for their home in the water. But, they thought, nothing they could do would make any difference. Nothing they could do would save them. So why, they thought, should they try?

Their despair had turned to apathy.

Except for one. She felt not in the least apathetic. She was young, she was pretty and she was passionate about life. 'And I have no intention of ending today as a fossil,' she thought.

So she cast about for the solution. And the answer arrived in the form of a boy and a dog.

At first, when she saw them crest the sand dunes, the young starfish was delighted. But there was a problem. How, surrounded by all her apathetic friends, was she to attract the attention of these potential sources of help?

The sun was rising. And the starfish could no longer scream – not even silently. Sprinkled across the beach, they looked like stars in a night sky, full of promise. But their eerie stillness showed how close to death they were.

Then, the dog bounded over to them causing much mayhem and some fear. At this point, the young starfish decided to take action. She waved with all her strength. And at last the dog noticed and came over. As he began to snuffle her sea-sparkling skin, she breathed in as deeply as she could. And then she blew out all the seawater and sand she had mustered.

The jet hit the dog square on the nose. He sprang back. This was the most exciting starfish he had ever found. He wanted to share his discovery with the boy. So, gently – with his great, soft mouth – the dog picked up the young starfish and took her back to the boy.

The boy was delighted. He gazed at the starfish, fascinated by her beauty. Then he had a thought. He flung the starfish as far out to sea as he could. And then picked up another . . . and another . . . and another . . . until he and his dog had returned hundreds of the sea-creatures to their home.

As she sank down through the gleaming green sea – with all her brothers and sisters following – the young starfish was glad she had taken such decisive action. And the moral of the story seemed to her to be: "When facing certain death, blow sand up a dog's nose!"

Some reflective questions:

For a manager

- Had the starfish any influence over factors creating their situation?

- Were the starfish right in their assumptions about their situation?

- What other attitudes could usefully motivate the starfish towards change?

- What was the young starfish's goal and what motivated her to achieve this?

- What personal resources did the young starfish have?

- Did she need external help and how could she access it?

- Is there a situation which you and your team now face which has induced apathy?

- Would you like to avoid foreseeable outcomes and what would motivate you to act?

- Do you need external help or are your personal resources sufficient to lead your team out of their apathy?

- What leadership qualities does the young starfish display?

- What leadership qualities do you have that could help in the current apathy-inducing situation and motivate your team towards change?

- Could a starfish strategy help you?

For a team

- Had the starfish any influence over factors creating their situation?

- Do you feel like that when you are at work?

- Were the starfish right in their assumptions about their situation?

- Are you right in thinking what you do about your work situation?

- What other attitudes might be helpful and what would motivate you to change?

- Is there a situation at work which you and your colleagues are facing which has induced apathy?

- What would motivate you to take action to avoid the possible outcome?

- Do you need external help or are your personal resources and those of your manager sufficient?

- If you need help, can you access it?

- What leadership qualities did the young starfish display?

- Would someone with these qualities inspire you in the current situation and motivate you to take action?

- How could a starfish strategy help you and your colleagues?

The Three Grains of Rice

*A traditional Indian story
re-told by Lisa Rossetti*

There was once a king who ruled his kingdom wisely and well. One day he called his three daughters together and told them he was leaving on a long journey. He gave each of them a gift to help them learn how to rule wisely.

Then he placed in each of their hands a single grain of rice. The first daughter tied a long golden thread around her grain of rice and put it in a beautiful crystal box. Every day she looked at it and reminded herself that she was powerful. The second daughter took one look at the common grain of rice and threw it away. The third daughter went outside and planted it in the ground. And it became a seed, giving life beyond itself, eventually turning into vast rice fields of hope and nourishment for others.

After many years the king returned and summonsed his three daughters. The king asked each daughter what they had done with their grains of rice. The first daughter said "I have treasured the grain of rice and kept it safe in this box."

The second daughter scoffed, "What was the point of giving me such a useless thing as one grain of rice?"

The king was very unhappy but he asked his third daughter what she had done. His daughter quietly took her father by the hand and led him to the palace window.

There before him stretched the vast fields of rice that had grown from one small grain. And the king saw people happily harvesting the crop together. Taking the crown off his head, he placed it on hers, saying:

"Beloved, you alone have learned the meaning of power contained in one small grain of rice."

From that day, the youngest daughter ruled the kingdom and all prospered.

Some reflective questions:

- What was the power in the grain of rice?

- What is this story about?

- For you, is this story telling us more about sharing our gifts (or talents) or about resource management? Both? Something else?

- What grains of rice are being thrown away in your team?

- What grains of rice are being kept within your team?

- What grains of rice are being nurtured within your team?

- How could you adapt this story for a modern workplace setting?

The Whispering

Hazel Bainbridge

"You don't want to do that now do you? It really wouldn't be a good idea would it?" There it was again, the Whispering voice from under the bed. Whenever he woke up it was the same. "What do you want to do that for, what would people think?" Even in the day it was there hiding round corners, "Don't do that, you might get it wrong". He pulled the pillow tighter over his head, buried his face into the bed, hoping the Whispering would go away.

Fingers of light began to play at the edges of the curtains. Soon they would stretch lazily across the carpet and the Whispering would be quietened. For a time. He wanted to get back to sleep but he couldn't and he really needed to go to the bathroom. Could he get out of bed or would the Whispering entangle his feet? In the end he stumbled across the hall in that bleary blur of not quite awakeness. And that is when the FIRST THING happened.

Whoosh! The toilet shot up and out of the roof with him sitting astonished on top of it. Once he had got his balance he began to look around. There was his house and his village. It all looked so small and so far away, like a toy town. What was going on? He breathed a deep breath and the Magic Toilet flew even higher, over the trees. It was warm up here, it was calm and peaceful.

He began to relax, things looked so different. He began to wonder how far he could go and what he could do. People didn't seem to be able to see him. He noticed if he took a deep breath he could fly higher and higher, and when he breathed out he moved closer to the ground. He could hover and float and he couldn't be certain but something else was different. And that's when the SECOND THING happened.

His lips began to twitch. He began to laugh. He was right... something else was different. The Whispering had stopped! He tried hard to hold the giggles in but they bubbled up and escaped, dancing excitedly out of his mouth. This was amazing. Up here everything seemed so simple. He was free. Without the Whispering he could have fun, he could fly anywhere he wanted.

It felt familiar and yet it couldn't be, could it? Was it real? Is this what it was like before the Whispering? Light as air.

Over the horizon the sun smiled and raised her head, her fingers spread out far and wide as she embraced the day. Birds sang, dew glistened and the day gently unfurled.

In his room a young boy slowly rubbed his eyes and pushed back the quilt. A smile played at the corners of his mouth. "RPK, it's time to get up" came the voice from downstairs. He stretched, jumped out of bed and bounced noisily down the stairs two at a time "Coming Mum!".

Inspired by Liam the
Accidental Traveller.

Some reflective questions:

- What would have to be true for you to have fun and treat each day as an adventure?

- How supportive is your inner dialogue?

- In what situations do you limit your potential by striving to meet the perceived expectations of others?

- What happens if you take a step back and look at the situation from a different perspective?

- If you were curious, really, really curious, what might be there right under your nose that you hadn't seen until now?

- Where would you go and what could you achieve if you believed it was possible?

The Wise Old Man and the Call Centre

Lizzie Gates

Once upon a time, a business manager had a bright idea. He imagined row upon row of workers, learning to 'smile down the telephone' and selling a huge range of products ranging from women's magazines to financial services. This work would be intensive and cost-efficient and the business manager could imagine huge profit – a veritable mountain of gold bullion sitting in his bank.

Thousands of other business managers agreed with him. And, together, they decided to name these clusters of workers 'Call Centres' and Call Centres sprang up all over the world.

But things did not work out well for the business managers. As they discovered, stress in the highly charged Call Centre atmosphere is a severe risk needing constant assessment. Staff turnover can be rapid, stress-related sickness absence, costly and sales figures, disappointing.

But, one day, a wise old man appeared. He had been providing travel services to travellers since the 1800s – the first were evangelical temperance supporters travelling by rail in 1841 – and the old man knew a thing or two about business. Even the post-9/11 travel industry crash – although it dented business for a while – had not seriously stopped the old man's corporate progress. So the business managers asked the wise old man to think about Call Centres. And he had another bright idea.

The old man's Call Centre was like no other. Because he was in the business of selling holidays, his Call Centre offices were travel-themed. This helped workers to tap into the best possible psychological state for selling holiday products. And each worker's positive and stress-busting experience began as soon as they crossed the threshold of his Call Centre.

Every day, whatever the weather or time of year outside the building, the old man's workers would walk across a bridge and immediately find themselves in a holiday atmosphere. Ocean music was playing, tropical palm trees and plants surrounded them and sand lay strewn on the ground. The experience sparked their imagination and creativity.

But the wise old business manager also motivated his call centre staff through fierce internal competition. His 500 workers were encouraged to communicate with each other and, as a result, everyone knew how well or badly everyone else was doing. Other motivating schemes involved teamwork, races and games. And the employee of the month – the one with the most sales to their credit – was publicly rewarded. Their team manager would serve them a cocktail as they lay on the faux beach of a faux Caribbean island in the faux sun in the centre of the huge open plan office floor.

The business moral of this story is: 'When seeking to engage and motivate staff, study them at play.' The old man's call centre workers were young but this approach of introducing imaginative environments and responsive employee care – even if not necessarily cocktails and team games – could work with others.

Some reflective questions:

For a manager

- What would success look like for the first call centre manager?

- What did it really look like in the light of experience?

- What do you want from your team? Greater success? More engagement – leading to greater success?

- How did the wise old man approach the problem?

- How might you make the working environment of your team more imaginative and engaging?

- What changes might suit them best?

- What might you do personally – as a team leader – to help your team achieve your objectives?

For a team

- What elements of management approach currently stress you?

- What does this look like – really?

- If your workplace was free of stress, how would you feel?

- How else might management demonstrate how much you are valued?

- What changes in your working environment might this involve – in an ideal world?

- What small steps might management take to organise your work in a more innovative and imaginative way?

- How might management develop your environment and work practices long-term to engage you and inspire greater productivity?

Your Choice

Denise Meakin

As a university academic, I sometimes work from home in order to have a silent space in which to spend time on tasks that require much focus and attention. Today is an intense day for me, working from home preparing an academic paper and marking student essays. Although I relish the opportunity to work from home from time to time, I am feeling lonely today. This is affecting my motivation and drive. Not having colleagues around with whom to share problems and issues is making me feel disconnected from the hub of my organisation, and my mind is filling with negative thoughts.

I carry on with my tasks regardless, with all the more negative thoughts infiltrating my concentration – "nobody cares about how hard I work... nobody notices that I'm doing all of this... how can I do all of this?" I start to feel more irritable. I pace around and slam the window shut, feeling a sense of satisfaction with my physical effort.

I glance at the ticking clock – it's almost midday and I have so much work to get through. More negative thoughts – "I must, I should, I haven't...".

The door to my home office squeaks open – I'm distracted from my irritability. I see Heather's beautiful enquiring eyes as her head peers around the door. "Let's play, Mummy", says my 8 year-old daughter. I need little encouragement as I take her hand and we hold our breath as we jump from the office desk, breaking the skin of the sea as we enter our new world.

We can breathe under the sea – we have magical lungs and feet with webbed toes. We swim, half walking and half doggy paddling, to a cave under the desk. It is here where we sit and look around at the shelves where books magically turn into colourful shoals of fish, where the foot stool elegantly dances as it transforms into a stunning sea urchin and where the sandy coloured carpet changes to a deep greenish hue before our eyes.

We look at each other and smile as we set off from the cave stroking the fish and watching them as they dart in and out of the book shelf crevices.

We can talk under the sea – we have a special dialect that only we and the sea creatures can understand. We cry with laughter at the clown fish and we ride on the back of sea horses who relish the opportunity to gallop through the water.

We rest on the giant sea urchin and eat our lunch of oyster pearl and seaweed sandwiches.

It's late – we've been here for hours and we must get back to the surface before the sea's skin turns hard and we can't get through. We make it just in time and clamber onto the desk for safety. We smile and hug.

Heather says "See you later, Mummy", as she exits the office door and dances to her bedroom. It's 12.20. I feel strangely calm yet re-energised. I set about my marking with a renewed sense of purpose and drive, feeling content as I hear Heather reading 'Jeremy Fisher' out loud in the distance. I am mindful of how my thoughts affect my feelings and how my feelings affect my actions. I have choices.

You have choices.

Some reflective questions:

- Do you notice when your team is de-motivated?

- Do you notice when your team need re-energising?

- How do you create time and space for your staff to 'play'?

Useful resources

Books – our top 20

We invite you to continue your learning in relation to story and storytelling. We provide you with a top 20 list below; it is not exhaustive by any means, but each of the books has impacted us on our journeys in some way.

If you think others should be added, please let us know!

Hooked: How Leaders Connect, Engage and Inspire with Storytelling - Gabrielle Dolan and Yamini Naidu (2013).

In Hooked, communication and business storytelling experts Gabrielle Dolan and Yamini Naidu use real–world examples and proven, effective techniques to teach the skill of great business storytelling and how to practice for perfection.

The Wise Fool's Guide to Leadership: Short Spiritual Stories for Organisational and Personal Transformation - Peter Hawkins (2005).

A traditional folk-tale hero. A modern spin on archetypal wise-fool Nasrudin's folk tales. The book also provides an introduction to Nasrudin and his stories, and a chapter on "Telling Tales; the positive use of stories in organisations."

The Power of the Tale: Using Narratives for Organisational Success - Julie Allan, Gerard Fairtlough and Barbara Heinzen (2002).

Includes company case studies to demonstrate how stories can build truth and trust, promote learning, develop skills, break new ground and create scenarios you can use in planning the future.

Storytelling in Organizations: From Theory to Empirical Research - Anna Linda Musacchio Adorisio (2009).

This book aims at studying life in organisations using a storytelling perspective. Storytelling is treated as a practice performed by organisational members and the emphasis is placed on the experience of such individuals.

Tales for Coaching: Using Stories and Metaphors with Individuals and Small Groups - Margaret Parkin (2010).

A guide to using extracts from literature, anecdote and metaphor to help coach staff, either individually or in groups. Tales for Coaching comes complete with 50 tales that managers can use immediately, ranging from Aesop through Stephen Covey to anecdotes the author has written herself.

Tales for Change: Using Storytelling to Develop People and Organizations - Margaret Parkin (2010).

Providing 50 tried and tested tales to aid change management, Tales for Change helps managers, trainers, educators and coaches to reinforce key messages and stimulate fresh thinking.

Lead with a Story: A Guide to Crafting Business Narratives that Captivate, Convince, and Inspire - Paul Smith (2012).

Complete with examples from companies like Kellogg's, Merrill-Lynch, Procter & Gamble, National Car Rental, Wal-Mart, Pizza Hut, and more, this practical resource gives readers the guidance they need to deliver stories to stunning effect.

The Magic of Metaphor: 77 Stories for Teachers, Trainers and Thinkers - Nick Owen (2001).

A "fable within a fable" anthology of powerful teaching tales and advice for telling them. Excellent and imaginative resource that will inspire creativity and guide its practical application.
Published over 10 years ago, but still a classic.

The Salmon of Knowledge: Stories for Work, Life, the Dark Shadow and OneSelf - Nick Owen (2009).

Intelligent exploration of tales to support personal development and understanding of others.

Magic of Modern Metaphor: Walking with the Stars - David Hodgson and Nick Owen (2010).

A thought-provoking book that both inspires and instructs in using story and metaphor. Bears witness to the incredible power of storytelling.

Fish Tales: Real Stories to Help Transform Your Workplace and Your Life - Stephen C. Lundin, Harry Paul & John Christensen (2003).

Engaging stories about how to transform the performance of teams. Structured and small enough for the busy manager to read in between meetings or on short lunch breaks.

Jonathan Livingston Seagull: A story - Richard Bach and Russell Munson (2003).

This is the classic self-awareness book from the 1970s – still uplifts and inspires. A wonderful example of the power of allegory to transform individuals.

Storytelling in Organizations: Facts, Fictions, and Fantasies - Yiannis Gabriel (2000).

Gabriel explores theories of organisational storytelling. With a section on using stories in organisations and how to understand culture through reflecting on modern myths and folktales arising in organisations.

Who Moved My Cheese? An Amazing Way to Deal with Change in Your Work and in Your Life - Spencer Johnson (1999).

This might have been published almost 15 years ago, but this is a classic story of the motivational genre. Well worth a read.

The Leader's Guide to Storytelling: Mastering the Art and Discipline of Business Narrative - Stephen Denning (2011).

Best-selling book, A Leader's Guide to Storytelling, uses illustrative examples and how-to techniques, and clearly explains how you can learn to tell the right story at the right time.

Tell to Win: Connect, Persuade and Triumph with the Hidden Power of Story - Peter Guber (2012).

Robust read with compelling stories of contemporary icons from the storied career of the former CEO of Sony Pictures.

The Secret Language of Leadership: How Leaders Inspire Action Through Narrative by Stephen Denning (2007).

Thorough exploration of the storytelling as a vital competency for modern leaders.

Squirrel Inc.: A Fable of Leadership Through Storytelling - Stephen Denning (2004).

In the Who Moved My Cheese idiom, this book introduces storytelling as a powerful force for leaders to motivate, engage and unite.

A Whole New Mind: Why Right Brainers Will Rule the Future - Dan Pink (2008).

Named Best Business Book of 2005. A useful introduction to developing creativity and innovation in oneself and as a source of business value. Particularly useful is the section on Story.

Drive: The Surprising Truth About What Motivates Us - Dan Pink (2011).

A refreshing exploration of what motivates us. In this paradigm-shattering book on motivation, Dan Pink explains that the secret to high performance and satisfaction in today's world is the deeply human need to direct our own lives, to learn and create new things, and to do better by ourselves and the world. Many illustrations and stories from those entrepreneurs and companies that are pointing the way.

LinkedIn Groups

LinkedIn has become a major professional networking medium for a huge array of discussion areas, from generalist to highly specialised. These discussions happen within LinkedIn Groups, which bring like-minded people together virtually.

There are many groups dedicated to story, storytelling, motivation, neuroscience, and so on. In terms of story, here is a list of LinkedIn Groups you might want to experiment with. Each has its own focus, such as health or marketing, so it is worth exploring which is the most suitable for your context.

As of August 2013, here is a sample of LinkedIn Groups related to story:

- Brand Storytelling

- Corporate Story Telling

- Friends of Center for Digital Storytelling

- Folktales (fairy tales)

- Narrative Coaching Network

- Reinvention Summit

- Health Story Project

- Organizational Storytelling

- Previsualization & Story Development Professionals

- Social Media Storyteller

- Social Storytellers: Online Video Storytelling & Strategy

- Story Driven Marketing

- Story-board Artist Café

- StoryTellers - The Oral History Group

- Storytelling as a healing art

- Storytelling for Business - hosted by Doug Stevenson

- StoryTHINKING and StoryTELLING

- Transmedia Storytelling

- Visionary Storytellers

Websites

A Storied Career – a curator website, with storytelling resources, articles, and interviews with organisational storytellers.

http://www.astoriedcareer.com

Anecdote Pty Ltd – offer courses and resources for Business Storytelling.

http://www.anecdote.com.au

GEECS - George Ewart Evans Centre for Storytelling.

http://geecs.tumblr.com/

Get Storied - US company specialising in personal branding online courses and resources, useful for small companies.

http://www.getstoried.com

Managerial Storytelling – research findings from Newcastle University Business School on the use of storytelling in management practice.

http://www.managerial-storytelling.com/

TED Talks – short online videos.

http://www.ted.com/topics/storytelling

Tim Sheppard - A wide range of articles and resources.

http://www.timsheppard.co.uk/story/tellinglinks.html

Organizational Storytelling Seminar Series – research and practice-based focus.

http://www.organizational-storytelling.org.uk

School of Storytelling (UK) – offers a course in organisational storytelling.

http://www.schoolofstorytelling.com

St Ethelburgas, London – storytelling workshops for mediation and community transformation.

http://www.stethelburgas.org

Accredited qualifications

>CWRS at the University of Chester, UK

The University of Chester's Centre for Work Related Studies in the United Kingdom has a unique negotiated, work based learning programme for professionals wanting to negotiate their own learning. This is a distance learning programme, so can be studied across the globe. Professionals can negotiate their award title around areas of:

- applied storytelling, for example: MA in Applied Storytelling for Health & Social Care, MA in Organisational Storytelling.

- leadership and management, for example: MA in Leadership & Performance Coaching.

- coaching and mentoring, for example: MA in Personal and Business Coaching.

Visit **http://www.cwrs.eu** or contact cwrs@chester.ac.uk for more information, quoting this book. Alternatively, you can contact Tony Wall (see his biography in this book).

LIBRARY, UNIVERSITY OF CHESTER

About the authors

Tony Wall

Tony Wall *BSc Hons BBA MSc MA PGCHE PGD ACIPD CMALT FHEA FRSA* is a specialist in personal and organisational transformation through work-based learning – using ideas from leadership, learning and applied psychology to help practitioners work through and rigorously investigate real world situations, leading to deeper, longer-lasting impact.

Tony works closely with businesses, training and educational organisations internationally to boost learning effectiveness through the university-accreditation of training courses – enabling learners to make bigger, longer-lasting, impacts at work – and at the same time – achieve prestigious university qualifications.

Tony speaks internationally on issues related to work-based learning and personal transformation. He has written and contributed to other books including *Leadership Assessment for Talent Development (2013)*, *Leading Transformation in Prior Learning Policy & Practice (2013)*, *Inclusive Higher Education (2013)*, *Transforming Prior Learning Policy & Practice (2012)*, *Learning Through Work (2010)*, and *Understanding Work Based Learning (2010)*.

t.wall@chester.ac.uk

Website: www.cwrs.eu

Link with Tony:
http://www.linkedin.com/in/cwrstony

Lisa Rossetti

Lisa Rossetti *BA Hons PGC PGD MA MAC* is an executive and leadership coach, writer and story practitioner. She currently works within health and social care settings for service improvement, CPD, recovery and wellbeing. Lisa writes about applied storytelling, creative writing and journaling for health and academic publications, including the NHS publication "Words for Wellbeing".

info@positivelives.co.uk

Website: www.positivelives.co.uk

Bob Meakin

Bob is a Senior Lecturer in the Centre for Work Related Studies, University of Chester. A linguist with thirty-seven years' experience teaching modern languages, English for Specific Purposes, communication skills and academic skills in the United Kingdom, France and the Middle East, Bob holds an enduring interest in the history and evolution of language, both spoken and written. He is continually reminded of the universal power of language as demonstrated by proverbs and metaphorical stories, yet fascinated by how variations in accent or dialects, and cross-cultural perspectives, can influence their effect and popularity.

r.meakin@chester.ac.uk

Website: www.cwrs.eu

Denise Meakin

Denise Meakin is a Senior Lecturer and leadership Accreditation Specialist at the Centre for Work Related Studies, University of Chester. She leads a unique work based learning facilitation programme recognised by the United Kingdom's Higher Education Academy. She speaks and writes internationally about how businesses and universities collaborate to enhance learning impact.

d.meakin@chester.ac.uk

Website: www.cwrs.eu

Hazel Bainbridge

Hazel Bainbridge has a passion for learning and adventures and enjoys a slightly irreverent view on life. She believes that getting what you want doesn't have to be hard and we can all be Transformers of our own experience. She works with leaders and managers to open their combination lock to success by identifying their inner strengths, unique talents and personal compass so they can embrace uncertainty and challenge with confidence. She has been coaching professionally since 2003, is accredited with the International Coach Federation and is a certified NLP (Neuro-Linguistic Programming) practitioner.

hazel@beingeffective.co.uk

Website: www.beingeffective.co.uk

Heather Meakin

Heather is a 16 year old student who will enter her first year of sixth form in September 2013, where she will begin her A levels. For the past two years, Heather has been in the process of completing her GCSEs and will receive the results of her hard work in August 2013. She has some lovely friends, who share her enjoyment for learning, most of the time. From a young age, Heather discovered her passion for horse riding. She has also always enjoyed story writing and has written many unpublished tales. Heather lives in the Cheshire countryside with her parents, her cat, Gwen, and her hamster, Pip. Animals have always been a large part of Heather's life, which is shown by her pet cemetery located at the top of her garden.

Lizzy Gates

Working in the UK and Europe, Elizabeth Gates MA has been a Language and Communication trainer for fifteen years. In 2005, she founded Lonely Furrow Company, a writing and communication consultancy, dealing with individual and corporate clients. Offering coaching, workshops and on-line training and assessments, she specialises in communication problems, using language and story to develop empathy and rapport.

elizabeth@lonelyfurrowcompany.com

Website: www.lonelyfurrowcompany.com

Peter Cook

Peter Cook is MD of Human Dynamics and The Academy of Rock – business development, better training, coaching and exceptional corporate keynotes and events. He is author of five books on business creativity and innovation, acclaimed by Professors Charles Handy, Adrian Furnham, Tom Peters and Harvey Goldsmith CBE.

Websites:

www.humdyn.co.uk

www.academy-of-rock.co.uk

Rob Jones

Now Equality and Diversity Manager for Cheshire West and Chester Council, Rob's background is in Human Resources in both the private and public sectors. A member of the Scout Association since 1974, and holding a range of leadership roles in the last 30 years, Rob enjoys most outdoor pursuits. Rob often uses his outside interests when at work – and he advises us that if you tell your team an outdoor pursuit is a management development exercise, it goes down better than calling it a Scout activity!

Vicky Evans

After 13 years working as a manager in large organisations, Vicky has worked for the last 10 years as a professional coach, helping hundreds of people to find and express their passions in their life and work. Her Creative Spark Workshop and Toolkit (www.creativesparktoolkit.com) support people who have an idea for a business but don't know how to take it forward. Vicky also works as a Visiting Lecturer in Business and Enterprise at the University of Chester. She is currently writing a book, "9 Little Devils", about the ways we stop ourselves doing the things we'd love to do and how we can resolve these patterns.

Website: www.creativesparktoolkit.com